But how do you get down the tree?

A Persian kitten's first outdoor expedition.

Paw fishing—a favorite sport of cats.

A comfortable observation post.

THE COMPLETE BOOK OF CAT CARE

How to Raise a Happy and Healthy Cat

37

Katrin Behrend Monika Wegler

Consulting Editor: Matthew M. Vriends, PhD

Expert advice for keeping cats with love and understanding.

BARRON'S

Contents

Practicing balancing. The rope really looks very sturdy, and you can always grab on with your claws to keep from plunging down before you're ready, and if worse comes to worst, Mother is nearby to save you.

◄ *Double spread on previous pages: Fishing cats. When the hunting drive is aroused and the prey is tempting, cats don't even avoid water, otherwise their least favorite element.*

More Happiness for Cats and People

Preface

All the things people say about cats would more than fill a book. Some praise their cuddliness, others prize their self-sufficiency, whereas others are convinced that independence and aloofness are the most notable characteristics of the cat's nature. In this book we have tried to regard the distinct character of the cat with entirely new eyes. We have had help from many longtime cat people. In preparation for this book we—the authors and the publisher—posed the question, "What would you like to know about cats?" It turned out that the greatest interest lies in the nature of the cat and its relationship to humans.

So here we have focused on the understanding of the diverse cat behavior patterns and handled all subjects from this point of view. You will learn, for example, which particular type of cat suits you, also whether an older cat can adapt to living with you, and what you should take into account in order to meet the requirements of a cat whose territory is limited to your home. Furthermore, the important questions about cleanliness, feeding, and maintaining health, the hotly debated subject of neutering, legal questions, behavior patterns, cat language, and living habits of outdoor cats are answered with competent advice and tips based on experience.

The pictures that photographer Monika Wegler took specially for this book are unique. Stimulated by the work of cat behavior researcher Paul Leyhausen, she has succeeded in presenting what the cat has to say to us in photographs that are powerfully expressive. Now you can read "graphically" and so understand your cat even better. The practical pages offer help for daily life with a cat, offering easy-to-follow guidance on equipment, care, feeding, health examination, birth, and development of kittens through pictures and concise text. The section on breeds presents prizewinning cats that fit our conception of beautiful, healthy animals. If you are a connoisseur of cats, you can test yourself with our "Kitten Identification Game" on the back cover flap. A glossary gives you cat facts from A to Z.

Every cat lover who reads this informative, beautifully illustrated, and entertaining guide will regard his cat with new eyes. The authors and the publisher wish you a good time with your pet.

Katrin Behrend
Monika Wegler

Opposite page: A picture-book cat. With her sea-green "storybook" eyes and white, fleecy coat, the chinchilla Persian is considered the unparalleled beauty of all cats.

The Cat—The Pet with a Past

The cat goes its own way. Even the manner in which it became domesticated was unique. As long as people were on the move as nomads, the cat kept its distance. But when they settled, when the Egyptians founded their kingdom and their grain stores were threatened by rats and mice, the cat approached humankind. It entered into captivity of its own free will, so to speak, enjoying the constant abundance at the table yet keeping its independence.

My cats have helped me write this book. They've been close by from the very first word. Matilda, for example, the handsome black house cat with the white medallion on her chest, usually dozes away her mornings on the soft comforter on my bed. Now she kept pattering up to me, and with soft, throaty chirpings laid her thick paws on my thigh and looked up at me out of her greenish-yellow eyes. Sometimes she sprang into my lap and stared, purring and blinking, at the growing lines of letters.

Or Nina, the graceful brown Burmese. Many times she jumped up, no, she soared up onto my desk, placed one foot carefully after the other between papers and the pages of opened books, and touched the clattering typewriter with a restrained gesture.

Yes, my cats have helped me. I sit at my desk every day, thus a circumstance that they are used to. But this time it was different. It had to do with them, and I was supposed to know that they knew this. And to pass it on to all who take pleasure in these extraordinary animals, who occupy themselves with them and want to learn to understand them better.

For there is one thing certain when you are dealing with a cat: It's the cat who determines the range of emotion from affection to withdrawal. Investigate this behavior, acquire understanding for it, and the foundation is laid for the proper cat-to-human relationship. And you will have many years with your cat, enjoying a happy and adventurous life together.

How Our Beloved Puss Developed from the Wild Cat

Statistics indicate that in recent years cats have overtaken dogs in popularity with animal lovers. The Pet Food Institute says that in 1985, 50 million pet cats inhabited 25 million homes in the United States; about 32 percent of all households in the United States now keep cats! This development makes sense to cat lovers, and a glance at past centuries shows that cats triumphed from the very beginning.

Worshiped as a Goddess
The cat took longer to become domesticated than any other of our house pets. Perhaps the reason for this was that as long as humans were nomadic, it didn't wish to attach itself to them. Only when they became settled and built houses did the cat draw closer to them.

Egypt, the mighty kingdom on the Nile, had established its entire state system on grain and bread. The wheat stores were warehoused in gigantic granaries, which were more and more beset by hosts of voracious rats and mice. And now the hour of the fallow cat was at hand. Until then it had lived wild in North Africa; now the abundant food supply attracted it. The cat attached itself to humankind and surrendered itself to captivity. Voluntarily. And the people recognized the uniqueness of this occurrence and made the cat into a goddess.

For along with the cat's highly prized ability to halt the incursions of rodents, which were feared as destroyers of grain stores and carriers of disease, people saw in her reserved, unfathomable nature something to be worshiped. So it wasn't much of a step to raise her to the status of an Egyptian goddess whose life was sacred. She was honored as the gentle, benevolent goddess Bastet, the Lady of Life, wife of Ra the sun god, and she was represented as a woman with the head of a cat. She had her own temples and burial grounds; it was a special honor to be able to bury one's "Mau," as the Egyptians called the cat, in the gigantic cemetery of Bubastis, the principal site of Bastet's cult. And anyone who did anything bad to his cat or even killed it was punished by death.

Persecuted as a Witch

Unfortunately, this state of affairs didn't last. Even though the Egyptians tried through strict regulation to prevent the cat from being taken out of the country, smugglers succeeded in taking her to Greece and ancient Rome. There her value as a mouse catcher was recognized very quickly and she was more favored than the weasels and snakes that had been kept for the purpose. Now the triumphal march of the cat throughout the whole of the then-known world was unstoppable. Everywhere she was regarded as something special; people marveled at her as an incomparable mixture of independent predator and gentle, affectionate creature, as well as at her talent as an indefatigable huntress.

But then her decline began. Around A.D. 1200, superstition was flourishing; the former goddess was demonized. The doom of the cat was that she remained unfathomable and mysterious and was connected with heathen practices. For 450 years she was tortured, burned, hanged, and stoned together with witches and heretics by the thousands. This pitiless hunt was to be terribly avenged. For because no one was restraining the rats now, they carried plague into the medieval cities and transferred it to humans through their fleas.

Whole cities and regions were wiped out and again, at first, people wanted to blame the cat because she thrived well in the plague regions—because of the rats.

Only when people discovered the real cause of the infection, at the high point of the plague in which millions of people died, did the cat come into favor again. Yet it took until well into the

Mother cat with her newborn. The little one must be cared for by his mother for twelve weeks. By then he is independent enough and can be taken home by his new owner.

9

It tastes better with two. Children love cats because of their soft fur, their affectionate natures, and their playfulness. Cats don't like to be forced at all, though, or to be grabbed clumsily and roughly. They determine when they are in the mood for contact. Children also should learn to respect the particular personality of a cat.

eighteenth century before her second ascent to popular house pet status began, an ascent that continues today.

Beloved as a Lap Animal

The contribution made by painters and poets to this ascent is not insignificant. The cat was promoted to artists' animal. She plays a leading role in numerous stories, for particularly among writers one finds partisan cat lovers whose partiality rests on the idea that cats are not bound by restrictions. It began with the tale of "Puss in Boots" by the Frenchman, Charles Perrault. This appeared in 1697 and portrayed the cat—that is, the tomcat—in an entirely new light. The witch's familiar turned into the helper of humankind. Country people, whom the cat had served as a mouser, had known this for a long time. Now the interest of the educated people and the nobility also was turned to the cat. In the middle of the eighteenth century, when hygiene entered the household with the discoveries of Louis Pasteur (he showed microbes to cause illness and plague and developed inoculations against them), people prized the cat even more as the symbol of spotless cleanliness. After the first cat show in London in 1871, after the founding of cat clubs in England and the United States in the waning years of the nineteenth century, and with the the beginning of systematic breeding of cats, the former "witch's beast" was, so to speak, rehabilitated. And so it is that the goddess Bastet with her small, high-eared head has turned into a lap animal that pleases us the same whether she is slender, fat, spotted, or plain, with a long-haired or wavy coat, primarily because she has remained true to herself.

A Low-Maintenance House Pet—Is This Really True?

When children talk about their cats the nicest things come out— and the most accurate. "A cat," a little boy declared to me, "has two sides, one soft and cuddly and the other sharp and pointed." The nature of the cat is Janus-headed. It will be out for itself even while it is seeking companionship. It will pursue its business as a hunter even as it cultivates contact with its people. It likes whipping through the garden or the house just as much as dreaming sleepily in its favorite spot.

Just have a taste of some of my yogurt.

What You Can Expect from a Cat

Judged by her behavior, the cat is a loner, but she doesn't want to forgo the society of other cats or humans. But the impulse must be hers. She passes many hours of the day sleeping or resting, goes her own secret ways, and also does not want to be bothered. To try to take her in your arms at such moments or to play with her would be quite wrong. She will either not respond at all or only unwillingly, possibly even scratching and biting, but if a cat is in the mood, so to speak, she can be really demanding, depending on her temperament. She will rub against your legs for a long time, jump into your lap, butt you with her head, or if you are sitting at a desk, sit in the middle of the paper until you do whatever it is she has in mind.

The rest is for you.

What the Human Must Do for the Cat

Whether you offer the cat a basket with a soft cushion for her rest periods doesn't make any material difference. Perhaps she won't use it at all but takes over your favorite chair or a sunshiny spot on the windowsill or a corner in a tiled bathroom because there's a hot-water pipe underneath it or, and this is by far the favorite, your bed.

Now just lick off my finger.

Of course, for the cat who is kept in the house, a scratching post on which the cat can sharpen its claws is a necessity; otherwise it'll do it on the furniture and carpets. Still better is a scratching tree on which the cat can enjoy its inclination to climb and do gymnastics.

A litter box is unavoidable. It should be in a quiet place, because the cat by its very nature wishes to be unobserved in "the quiet place." And if you don't take care to keep the place utterly clean, the cat will indicate emphatically what it thinks of an unclean litter box that smells of cat excrement. I have had the experience of finding a protest left in the freshly washed laundry or in a wastebasket. There are of course other things that are part of the proper maintenance of a cat. You will find all the details of

A favorite resting place. Only a cat could manage to lie so relaxed and at ease in the most uncomfortable of places. It passes a major portion of the day sleeping and resting and does not care to be disturbed then.

what to do to keep your cat contented, healthy, and cheerful in the chapters that follow.

Of the Soothing Nature of the Cat

When my daughter was still small, she once said to me very happily, "I'm glad we have Nina. Whenever I cry, she comes and nuzzles me so that I feel better. The nice thing is, she does it when I holler, too."

It's said that cat owners live more healthily and longer than other people. Even if there's no scientifically based evidence for this, there are still some grounds for it. The relationship between cats and people exists mainly because they are mutually soothing. The cat keeper likes to hold his pet, stroke the soft, smooth fur, bump his nose against the cold cat nose, scratch the delicate little ears. The cat loves to stretch out along the human legs, rub its head against his hand, curl up on his lap. This friendly contact enables the human to deal with stress, grow calm, and relax.

Another reason is the fact that the cat is, although repeatedly and erroneously said not to be, candid and direct in its relations with humans. What it wants, it expresses, and you can rely on that.

Also cats, by their nature, can be extraordinarily comforting for old people. They are company for loneliness, are not importunate and stressing, can be cared for without difficulty, and radiate infinite peacefulness when they purringly nestle against a person. "A gentle therapist" they were called by one cat lover, and I find that is not an exaggeration.

Getting a Cat

I had the following experience with my first cat: We were on vacation with Italian friends in a remote house in the Apennines. One morning our dog Willy was growling and barking in front of a pile of boards and getting terribly excited. When we investigated, we discovered a tiny kitten, scarcely more than six weeks old. Where the little creature came from remained a mystery to us. No neighbors far and wide, no mother cat anywhere that was looking for her lost kitten. So we adopted Meow-Meow, just as she had adopted us.

This rather odd way of getting a cat happens more often than you'd think. The normal way, however, is to decide ahead of time to get a cat and then to carefully look for one. For there are cats and cats, and there are many ways for you to choose the right one.

What Cat Is Right for You?

You're a person who works at a demanding job all day long. When you come home in the evening you want some peace and quiet. Your cat on the other hand has just been waiting for the moment you return and now literally throws herself at you. She, of course, wants to play and romp, is loud and spirited, whereas you want to quietly enjoy your evening at home.

This example should show you how important it is to pay attention to type and disposition when you're getting a cat. Of course it's not very easy to tell about temperament right off, because every cat meets you with reserve at first. The descriptions and advice that I give on the following pages, based on my own experience and long observation, offer no claims to infallibility. Bear in mind that the cat is imprinted by many influences: the mother, the milieu from which it comes, the characteristics of its breed if it is a purebred cat (see Portraits of Favorite Purebred Cats, pages 116 to 137), and the environment in which it will live. This means that a cat that lives only in the house will develop differently from one that has the run of the yard or lives entirely free, like a farm cat. So don't be disappointed if your puss ultimately develops differently. Precise diagrams simply are not possible with such a complex living creature.

The Friendly Cat
In general, this cat does not exhibit any particular shyness toward people. After a short period of reserve it will come to you in a friendly way and allow itself to be stroked and its head scratched.

Shady lookout tree. From here it has a good view over everything, and also can endure heat with a little panting.

13

What's moving there? A kitten who has experienced loving attention from humans from the beginning views the world with trust and will approach unknown "play-things" openly and curiously. Of course you should keep cats from playing with houseplants. This isn't good for either the plants or the kittens, because some plants are poisonous (see page 45).

It also can demand this devotion and will take its place on your lap as if it were a matter of course. It is curious, active, and playful and gets along very well with children as long as they don't roughly pull its tail.

My tip: Even the cat that likes contact detests being taken for granted. Wait until it comes on its own for affection or play.

The Timid Cat

It is reserved by nature and keeps its distance for a long time. At its first meeting with you, it will at first withdraw into a hiding place and do its observing from there. It then cautiously makes contact with you, but when the ice is broken, this cat bonds especially devotedly to "its" people. But it will always remain shy toward others. You must not let this cat down, because it will recover only with difficulty.

My tip: You must not rush this cat. Perhaps it's the smallest of its siblings, and just for that reason you've lost your heart to it. Now you must practice patience and show it with "treats" that it comes first with you.

The Serene Cat

Cat lovers who are inclined to be contemplative will bond with this type. This puss is even tempered and shows itself to be tolerant in the circle of its cat siblings. It takes its time with new contacts, not because it is afraid but because it sniffs everything calmly and never hurries for anything. It is the ideal companion on trips for it can spend hour after hour in its basket with feet tucked under without yowling. It doesn't suffer under stress, for it appears not to let itself be affected at all.

My tip: A serene cat stays its ground, that is, it doesn't withdraw to observe. If you recognize this small difference, you will know whom you are dealing with.

The Capricious Cat

Perhaps we should rather describe this type as touchy and sensitive. They love to take offense and then can "pout" for hours. And woe to anyone who contests this cat for the place it has just selected for itself. Then it has a store of tricks that very quickly make clear who is boss here. Besides, it is fearful and nervous and is not suitable for loud people.

My tip: Such characteristics are rather typical of certain breeds (see Portraits of Favorite Purebred Cats, pages 116 to 137). Give careful thought ahead of time to what you value more, the outer appearance or the disposition (see Purebred Cats from a Breeder, page 19).

Some Observations About Coat Color

This is always being linked with the temperament of the cat. There even have been attempts to establish scientifically that black cats are affectionate, black-and-whites love to play, the red ones like quiet, wild-colored ones need freedom, and white cats are said to be sensitive. These ideas are not without dispute in expert circles, and so it's up to you to make your own observations and draw your own conclusions.

Perhaps you'll be interested in this correlation: that how cats have dispersed over the world can be read through the percentage distribution of coat color. So, for example, the orange cats from Asia Minor and North Africa were supposed to have gone by sea to Great Britain and Germany, black cats to be strongly represented in northwestern England, in Morocco and Algeria. The striped ones spread from England out through the Rhone valley to the Mediterranean, and in Manhattan there are just as many black-and-whites to be found as there are in Amsterdam. Of course the island of Manhattan was settled by the Dutch. They were later driven out by the British, but their cats remained.

How To Find a Cat

If you get a cat you should realize that for the next 12 to 15 years you will be dealing with a self-willed personality. Therefore, if possible, you should choose your new companion with care.

The Sweet Kitten Nursery

When your friends or neighbors have a litter of kittens, you have the best opportunities for choice. Here you can spend ample time with the individual kittens and finally choose the one that suits you best. You see how the mother cat is cared for by the people and

"Dance" with a mouse. The fluffed-out tail fur shows that the cat is looking away with only sham boredom. Yet it is trembling with excitement and hunting zeal.

Playing hide-and-seek combined with tag. This way kittens learn to use patience later in front of a mouse hole. They crouch opposite their opponent, lie in wait, dare to make a feinting attack, and at the right moment dart forward and grab.

how she behaves toward them. Such things, though they may appear incidental to you, have an enormous effect on the character of the kittens. You can rely on the following:

- If the mother cat sought the protection of humans before and during the birth, she has trust and will communicate it to her kittens.
- At intervals of about ten to 14 days you can follow the development of the kittens and thus get a picture of the individual types. For example, see how they behave in the tussle to get at the source of milk, how the kittens play with each other, how they manage the trips to the litter box, and whether they are shy of visitors (see page 14).

◄ *Double spread on previous pages: Acrobat on the garden fence. The cat's dreamlike certainty as it jumps from one board to the next is wonderful.*

- Don't let your choice be influenced by the coat color alone. Try to learn something about the nature of the animal. Thus you usually can figure that from a bold kitten that is not hand shy will develop a self-confident lively cat. Even so, let it be said first off that in many instances a timorous little creature will develop into a fine, reserved cat that relates exclusively to one person. Of course—you never can be certain there won't be surprises.

Purebred Cats from a Breeder

Not only must you pay a good deal of money for one of these, but you must also decide on a very specific type, which is primarily determined by looks. Even so, not every cat is right for every person. Persian cats, for instance, are said to be comfortable and calm; Siamese on the other hand are reputed to be lively, always "talking," and intent on close contact with their people. Thus it's better to study the descriptions of the individual breeds first and then make a choice (see Portraits of Favorite Purebred Cats, pages 116 to 137). In addition there's grooming to consider, for long-haired cats like the Persians must be combed and brushed every day or their fur snarls. You also should bear the following things in mind when buying a purebred cat:

- It's best to buy from the breeder. Pet stores and possibly veterinarians can supply addresses. You also can ask organizations of breeders of pedigreed cats or clubs for the particular breed (see Addresses and Literature, page 141) about known litters of the various breeds.
- If you want to have a cat that is classified as a "show cat" or "suitable for breeding," you usually must wait a long time for it and pay the highest price for it..
- Kittens that do not conform precisely to the desired Standard (see page 114) in form or color are considered "pet animals." They are then not suitable for breeding and are sometimes available more cheaply from breeders or pet stores.
- Adult purebred cats are often quite different in appearance, especially in coat color and markings, from kittens. You should know this when you've fallen in love with an especially sweet kitten. Look at the photographs in the breed portraits (see pages 116 to 137)—these show both kittens and adult cats—and take the advice of the breeder about it.
- It's instructive to visit a large cat show. There you'll get into conversation with many cat breeders and fanciers and can learn a great deal.
- When taking delivery of a purebred cat you've bought, you should have:

1. the pedigree certificate; it must contain the name and color of the ancestors for four generations and show that the animal has been registered with the appropriate authority such as the American Cat Association (ACA) or Cat Fanciers' Association (CFA). A transfer certificate to register the change of ownership

Turkish Van cat at the garden pond. The cat is very lively, dashes around a great deal, and—very untypically for a cat—likes to go swimming (see page 123).

Twelve-week-old Burmese cats (lilac and chocolate) at play. What always appear to humans as disarmingly comic routines are learning games for small cats. They train their muscles and practice to control their movements and to defend themselves against an attacker with paws, claws, and teeth.

must be filled in and sent to the appropriate authority once the sales is completed.

2. the certificate of immunizations; this contains information about the shots against feline distemper (infectious enteritis or panleukopenia), feline "cat flu" mainly caused by one of the two feline respiratory viruses—feline herpes virus (FVR) and feline calcivirus (FCI), and rabies. Only a cat intended for breeding can already have had the first inoculation against leukemia (see Inoculations, the Best Precaution, page 60).

• Find out whether the cat has been wormed.

Cats from the Pet Store

Who hasn't been caught in the pet store when they see the kittens romping around in clumsy bravery. Before you can get away, you've lost your heart to the cheeky little tricolored one with the black pirate patch over one eye and want to buy it. Because such kittens are usually purebred, caution is indicated and not only in the matter of price. You shouldn't act hastily in any case but proceed with exactly the same caution as I have already described. Look the store over well. A good pet dealer will keep his cats clean, furnish them with opportunities for play and for cuddling, and provide them with the right diet as well as the necessary attention. Besides, he will give you as much help as possible in making your choice.

Cats from the Animal Shelter

The desire to give a new home to an abandoned or masterless animal is not the only good reason for choosing this avenue. There are also a couple of solid considerations that should be weighed in a decision to get an older cat.

Being ready to leap, attack, and defend oneself is part of a kitten's daily practice. Whoever gets to sit on top always has the best overall view. And if it gets boring, one can start the next fight.

- You're still young, have just begun your profession, and don't know what sort of changes life has in store for you. With a young kitten, you must plan on undertaking responsibility for an average of 15 years. With an older cat you shorten this time period.
- You still have very small children but would like them to grow up with an animal. Here a younger adult cat is recommended. It should be accustomed to much social contact and be nice and gentle. A cat like this is able to defend itself against the impetuous grasp of small hands without scratching and biting (see What Cat Is Right for You, page 13).

Availability: Currently, homeless cats are available not only from animal shelters but also some pet stores and private persons undertake responsibility for this service. Don't let yourself be given any cat that is not inoculated and wormed and provided with the appropriate proof. The more precisely the supplier inquires how and where the cat will be kept, the more you can trust him. It shows that he is interested primarily in the comfort of the cat (see Addresses and Literature, page 141).

Note: Such cats sometimes have been through a great deal and can be difficult. Be very sure you realize that you must use a great deal of affection and patience with an animal like this in order to reestablish its lost trust (see Acclimation—A Matter of Temperament, page 28).

Cats from Newspaper Advertisements

Unfortunately, ads found under the rubric "Animal Market" conceal a variety of interests.

- Cat lovers who really only want a good home for kittens. Many will give up the kittens free, but then they already should have provided for the inoculations and the worming and be reimbursed for these outlays.
- Entrepreneurs who allow their cats to be bred for money, and this as often as possible. They ask for a cover charge—which simply means the selling price—and usually have not had these kittens immunized.
- Owners of purebred cats who are giving up so-called "pet animals" (see page 19).
- Breeders who pursue the business professionally. You can learn precise details from a purebred-cat organization (see Addresses and Literature, page 141). Breeders entered there operate under strict rules.

Stray Cats

Perhaps it happens to you the way it did to me in the story I told. Usually a cat will wander around your house meowing and begging for food. Not every one of these cats is homeless, however. There are animals that, for whatever reason, always literally swing back and forth between two homes. If they appear to be cared for and well nourished, you may be dealing with a cat that likes to "serve" two masters. Not only should you always ask around the neighborhood to find out if an animal is missing. You should report to the animal shelter that you've found a cat and give the tattoo code (see page 38), if there is one. How happy you can make the cat owner who thinks he's lost his kitty.

Even so, a cat that has arrived on your doorstep may not be homeless. You should try every means to discover the owner. This can take a while, of course. Try to win the trust of the animal by giving it food regularly. As soon as it will let you handle it, have it inoculated and wormed by the veterinarian.

An impressive purebred cat face. Persian with odd eyes.

Two Cats Are Better Than One

Of course it's said that the cat prefers to live alone, but stop a moment and consider its situation, especially in an apartment. A secure roof over its head, warm, comfortable sleeping spots, a constantly filled food bowl, a territory that no one disputes—where's the challenge, from the cat's point of view? Some cats are regular loners. They bond very closely to their humans and don't want to share with any other animal. Others, on the other hand, miss social contacts, and they suffer from boredom. Especially if you are heavily involved in your job, I would advise you to have a second cat.

Possibilities are:
- two siblings from one litter: Observe them so that you can find out which ones get along well together;

- an older and a younger cat: Choose them so that the new one's temperament complements that of the older inhabitant;
- two grown cats: Get them used to each other with much tact and intuition and offer them enough space in the apartment so that each one can establish its own territory (see Old Pet and New Cat—A Sensitive Subject, below).

The Siamese cat (Cream point, eleven weeks) is restless, lively, and always ready to play. It is very devoted and only suitable for people who have much time.

Female or Male?

I've had both but for the life of me cannot express any recommendation. My first cat Meow-Meow, the foundling cat imported from Italy, was self-willed and moody and used to urinate while standing, like a tomcat. Nina, the Burmese, is the absolutely proverbial pet cat. Morellino, the tomcat, showed his love with upsetting vehemence, and Matilda, who is large and stately like a tomcat, throws herself on a person and purrs noisily and full of ardor. Do these descriptions tell you anything about sex? I don't think so. Nevertheless, consider beforehand:

A female is sexually mature between the sixth and twelfth month of life and then is in heat—that is to say, ready to mate— two to three times a year. If she has freedom to roam, she can have kittens every time. If kept in the house, where she will not ordinarily meet a tomcat, she will remain in the mood for love, at high volume, for ten days, sometimes even as long as two to three weeks, which is a very strenuous circumstance for both the observers and for the cat herself, plus not being exactly good for her health.

A male becomes sexually mature at the age of 9 months and then marks his territory by spraying urine everywhere. In the house it smells dreadfully.

My tip: If you have the animal neutered, this problem is avoided from the outset (see page 35).

Old Pet and New Cat—A Sensitive Subject

An old pet—be it dog or cat—and a new kitten is a situation that you must handle by intuition. Unfortunately it can't be said that it always works out harmoniously. In any case you should carefully respect the feelings of the older inhabitant and not let it feel that you are giving preference to the new one just because it's young and sweet.

A cat that has hitherto been the only animal in the household and was at the center of things will suffer very much when you don't give it the same attention because of the new arrival. It may react with behavior disturbances, for example, not eating anymore or doing its business in the middle of the carpet (see When the Cat Suddenly Stops Being Housebroken, page 34). So don't let it miss its usual attention and be careful to provide enough places so that the two can get out of each other's way. Feed the new one in a different place and set up a second litter box far away from that of the original inhabitant.

A dog can be induced to accept the new pet, even if it has been in the family for a long time (see Meeting Other Pets, below). With Willy, our mutt, I was helped by the fact that we were just moving into a new house. I took the kitten inside first and then let the dog in. And voila, it worked. Willy accepted the hissing, spitting bundle of the cat as dominant over him and from then on she ruled as queen.

Meeting Other Pets

Of course you can have a cat with other pets. When misunderstandings arise, they usually are caused by ignorance of the different behavior patterns of the individual animals. Cats will have no fear of animals that are smaller than they are, but they may possibly view them as delicacies or playthings. However, animals that are the same size or larger will be considered enemies, at least until the cat is convinced of the contrary. Nevertheless, at first you must make sure that neither security, nor rank, nor territory is threatened.

Dog: The so-called hereditary enmity between dog and cat is a folktale. Still, there are cats that can't stand dogs and vice versa. Often these simply are difficulties in understanding. In a dog, a wagging tail means a friendly, interested gesture of approach, whereas in the cat it is a negative signal of rage, ill humor, excitement, and aggression. If the dog raises his foot, he wants to play, whereas the cat uses this as a gesture of threat.

Things go well:

- when two animals are raised together from babyhood; they are used to each other and "understand" each other;
- when a grown-up dog is exposed to a young kitten, which I must limit by saying that it depends on the particular breed of dog (hunting dogs and watchdogs are not friendly to cats, as a general rule); good-natured and well-trained dogs can be taught that from now on the cat belongs to the pack. Things go only limitedly well or not well at all when a young dog is brought into a situation with an adult cat who has been "the only child." The cat can be depressed to such an extent that it turns into an anxious, unhappy animal that constantly creeps into hiding.

Guinea pigs and hamsters: Cats can become friends with guinea pigs, but you shouldn't rely on it. Hamsters probably will be seen as prey.

Dwarf rabbits: Depending on the temperament of the cat, you can accustom the two to each other. Watchfulness and much patience are necessary in any case.

Budgerigars and canaries: Cats hunt birds and eat them. Even here, as stories are always showing, exceptions prove the rule.

Parrots and larger parakeets: They can become jealous and injure the cat with their beaks; on the other hand it can claw and bite them.

Opposite page: Cat on a visit. It may look that way, but watch out! A dog who is supposed to watch house and yard naturally also will regard a cat as an intruder and will chase it.

Everthing the Cat Needs
On these pages you'll find all the equipment a cat needs.

Cat Basket
Picture 1
For resting and sleeping the cat needs a place where it will be undisturbed. A basket, like the one pictured here, offers it protection and

1) The cat needs a basket for a secure place to rest and sleep.

privacy at the same time. Put a washable cover on the cushion and put the basket in a warm, draft-free spot where it can always remain. It may happen, of course, that your cat will choose another spot for its favorite and never use the most comfortable basket in the world.

Litter Box
Picture 2
The litter box is essential, even if the cat has access to the outdoors, when it will be living on the land and will do its business outside for the most part. Litter boxes are sold in pet stores in various designs.

A simple plastic tray is good, also for taking on trips.

2) The litter box should be placed in a quiet, protected spot.

The plastic tray with a removable rim is very practical. The cat litter doesn't get spread around quite so much with the cat's scratching. The little house with a drawer is even cleaner, because there are cats that urinate standing up.

Use the litter especially formulated for cats. It reduces odor and must of course be guaranteed to be asbestos free (read the contents!). Obtainable in bags of 10 to 50 pounds.

Environmental Tip: The pet stores now offer a biodegradable cat litter that is free from any chemicals and dyes and, being a pure natural product, can be thrown on the compost heap. Remove feces first.

Grooming Utensils and Toys
Picture 3

For grooming: A comb and brush are needed for grooming the coat. Short-haired cats only need brushing during the shedding season so they don't swallow too much dead hair. Long-haired cats, on the other hand, need regular grooming or the fur will mat and combing becomes torture. You need the following:

For short-haired cats
- one rubber brush (see picture) or one brush with natural bristles, firm but not too hard;
- one chamois coth, which gives the coat the final polish.

3) Combs and brushes, ball and mouse are essential for the cat's comfort.

For semi-long-haired and Persian cats
- one brush with bent-wire bristles;
- one metal comb with coarse teeth;
- one metal comb with fine teeth;
- one seam-cutting knife for removing knots in the fur.

For playing: The pet store's offerings range from all types of mice to balls to bones for gnawing and many more. Only

4) A cat can become accustomed to walking on a leash.

5) The cat should be able to stand up to the scratching post.

6) There certainly are different tastes in every friendship.

7) Cats are very fond of the small leaves of the umbrella plant.

get hard rubber balls; I advise against foam rubber balls, because cats will chew and eat them. You also can provide empty thread spools, corks, empty cartons, or paper bags.

Cat Harness
Picture 4
It doesn't hurt for a cat to get used to walking on a leash, even if it doesn't learn to "heel" like a dog. Most practical is the cat harness, which goes around the chest and belly and doesn't threaten to choke the cat when it pulls very hard against the lead. A collar with an address tag for cats who are exploring their neighborhood without supervision should have an elastic section

so the cat won't strangle if it gets hung up on something.

Scratching Post
Picture 5
The cat needs a scratching post for sharpening its claws. It must be sturdy or the cat will have it in ribbons in no time and will then return to rugs and furniture. Best is a post wrapped with coarse sisal hemp. It should be nailed at a height that allows the cat to stand up to it.

Food and Drinking Dishes
Picture 6
They should be as heavy and stable as possible, best made from glazed pottery. It's advisable to place them on a mat because the cat "mucks

up" its surroundings when eating. Two dishes are needed, one for food and one for water. For Persians it's better to use a very shallow dish.

Cat Grass
Picture 7
Cats need "greenery," perhaps to help them vomit up hair balls. Indoor cats prefer to make do with houseplants. But a whole long list of those are poisonous (see page 44). So accustom your cat to grass, which can be bought at the pet store in a container. They also like umbrella plant and spider plant. Be sure that the leaves are soft and supple. Cats can suffer injury from the older, sharp-edged ones.

Living with a Cat

Living with a cat means getting used to its contradictory nature. At one moment a gentle animal with soft, caressive fur, velvet paws, graceful movements, and affectionate ways, the next moment she is aloof, unresponsive to the feeling the human is offering her. In dealing with cats you have to adjust to this alternation between approach and withdrawal.

I think sometimes that I'd like to be a cat living with me, as I watch my two all day long. They can spread out at any time in the most comfortable place, regularly get their food and petting whenever they want it. Clearly they seem to believe that humans were created for their comfort. This is only a surmise, of course. On the other hand it is certain that you'll live even better with the cat if you know how, for example, it wins its territory, behaves toward other pets, or settles dominance ranking with another cat. You'll also find answers here about all matters of cleanliness, training, and avoidance of hazards.

Acclimation—A Matter of Temperament

Finally you've made your choice. Fetch your new housemate in a cat carrier, preferably in the car and with two people. Then one person can talk soothingly to the animal on the trip. At home, set the carrier in its place and open the door. Now the acclimation phase begins. If you've already spent some time with the animal, the way I've outlined in the last chapter, you already know its disposition.

When the Cat Is Young
It's best if you allow the kitten, which should not be younger than 12 weeks, to explore the room quietly on its own for the first time. The area must of course be free of hazards (see page 44). Put the litter box in with it, also a shallow dish of food that the kitten is used to (obtained from the previous owner) and a dish of water. Crouch beside the cat carrier and call the kitten softly by its name. Certainly it will be meowing for its mother and siblings to come to it. If you answer with a gentle voice, it will slowly learn to know you and to trust you.

My tip: If there are no dangers at all to threaten the kitten, you can comfortably leave it in the room overnight. As soon as it has lost its fear of its new surroundings, it will no longer retreat into its hideaway.

When the Cat is Older

In principle, the acclimation is no different from that of the young kitten. Still, because the cat already has been imprinted with its former environment, you must take that into consideration and adapt accordingly.

The anxious cat: Possibly it has had a bad experience with humans. Try to find out what it's afraid of. This could be movement, sounds, or much hubbub in the family. Perhaps you already have another pet, a dog or a parrot, of which it is afraid. Don't pressure it and always allow the cat to withdraw into a hiding place. It needs much calmness and should not be frightened by sudden approaches. This will only make it shier.

The difficult cat: Only much love and patience (see Cats from the Animal Shelter, page 20) will help. This cat scratches and bites when you try to touch it. Don't reach for it, regularly give it its food, and always treat it the same way. Gradually it will learn to know you and perhaps to trust you.

It is also difficult for a cat to get used to new people when it is over ten years old. It has become so close to its master or mistress that it just sneaks off and hides and threatens to starve from homesickness and grief. Here homeopathic remedies, which have a rebuilding effect, may help. Get the advice of a veterinarian with experience in homeopathic treatment of animals.

Approach with caution. It doesn't seem to be so terribly uncanny to these two. Because the rat never has encountered a cat before, it approaches without any constraints. And tomcat Robin has learned that he may not hunt animals that live with him.

Establishing Territory

Domestic cats can be divided into three categories, according to the circumstances under which they live:

- Indoor cats. Their territory is the house and perhaps there is even a terrace at their disposal.
- Outdoor cats. In addition to the humans' house they can enjoy a yard, or a courtyard, or in the best case, the whole outdoors. From this point of view indoor cats are at a disadvantage. Still, you can take some measures so that their behavior patterns, which they carry over from outside to inside, aren't too severely limited.
- Farm cats. They live in the stable and barn and outside in free nature.

The primary home: This is the calm pole in the cat's life, usually a room or even a corner in an area of the house in which it lives. It seeks it out quite soon after it has gotten to know the house and passes many hours a day there. Nina, a very dainty cat, found the small heating unit in the kitchen exactly the right place for her. Since we moved, she occupies a similarly warm place, this time the windowsill behind my desk. From there she also can spring into the middle of my work from time to time and establish contact with me. Matilda used to like to sit on top of the cupboard in the kitchen. In the new apartment she wavered at first between the broad sofa back and my husband's bed. Since we got a new sofa, she now spreads out on the bed exclusively (see What the Cat Should Learn, page 40).

Maternal solicitude. The six-week-old kitten has climbed up and meows piteously. At this age, climbing down backwards doesn't work so well. So Mother must help. Afterwards she licks the youngster from stem to stern for reassurance.

The territory: This consists of the rest of the house and everything that belongs to it, that is, deck, terrace, or roof. Here the cat strolls around, plays, meets with other inhabitants, for instance a second cat, or seeks out a hideaway. Obviously there are territorial boundaries at which the one cat gives another right of way. In this case they each greet each other with a touch of the nose and tail held high.

A Home to a Cat's Taste

A cat that shares a one-room apartment with its person can have at least as interesting a life as one that has several rooms at its disposal. In the cat's view, it's diversity that provides excitement. It goes without saying that dangers that can threaten the cat in its explorations should be avoided (see Dangers to Cats, page 44).

Space requirements: For the cat an area that it can observe entirely without moving from one spot is dull and, in the long run, boring. Perhaps the space can be divided up so that there are interesting, attractive recesses and niches in it. Even more entertaining are several rooms, including kitchen and bath. They can be inspected over and over, and the cat is thus encouraged to move.

Furniture: Cats that can go outside seek places that are warm, dry, closed on two sides, and high if possible. So let something like this be set up in the house. In the pet stores there are various models of scratching and climbing trees with plat-

forms for sitting and caves for cuddling in arranged at various heights. If you're handy with tools, you can create such an arrangement according to your own taste.

- Wrap the supporting column—a round or rectangular piece of wood (can be bought in a builder's supply or garden center, garden post section) or a thick, branching limb—with sisal hemp.
- Boards fastened at different heights invite the cat to sit.

Embellishments: This of course also applies to ready-made climbing trees.

- With a thick sisal rope the cat can balance on it or do gymnastics (see photographs, pages 4 and 5).
- Tinfoil balls, little pieces of fur, and colored ribbons suspended on rubber bands invite play. Also exciting for indoor cats are cartons that they can open themselves and climb into, boxes that are upside down under which they can hide, and out-spread newspapers with which they can scuffle. The important thing is variety.

Cleanliness—No Problem

The cat has a reputation for being the model of cleanliness. Not only does it use the litter box on its own, once it has been trained properly, but it also carefully buries its urine and feces, as if seeing to it that we are not bothered by their odors. What can be more convenient for the person who is concerned about the cleanliness of his home?

Concealing its leavings is not an inborn characteristic, however, but a sign of dominance ranking (see Queen in Her Territory, page 94). Dominant, free-living cats leave their feces uncovered in the most noticeable place possible as a "scent threat." On the other hand, friendly cats or those of lower rank bury theirs. Therefore, the conclusion follows, they also do it in their life together with humans, provided it's harmonious and free of disturbances (see When the Cat Suddenly Stops Being Housebroken, page 34). To keep it that way at all times, you need to observe a few requirements.

Place for the litter box: Bathroom or quiet, protected place.

Maintaining cleanliness: Fill with cat litter 1 to 1½ inches (3 to 4 cm) deep. Remove feces and damp litter daily with a scoop and shake in some fresh litter. With a cat that's healthy and well kept, it's enough to remove all the cat litter once a week, placing it in a plastic bag and putting it in the trash. Don't put it in the toilet! Rinse out the litter box with hot water. Don't use detergent or disinfectant because cats can't "smell" it and may possibly reject their litter box. Wipe it dry and fill it with fresh litter.

Litter box for several cats: Two cats excite each other to more frequent use of the litter box. Why this should be so I don't know, but you must take it into consideration and either change the litter more often or even start out having a second litter box.

Opposite page: Catch the mousie. The child and her Siamese cat show loving understanding of each other. The cat reaches toward the quietly offered toy with a careful gesture.

Easy prey. Keeping cats and birds together usually doesn't work well. In any case, the cage must not be so easily accessible to a cat with a skillfully wielded paw but should be hung or placed in an unreachable spot.

When the Cat Suddenly Stops Being Housebroken

Your cat has been good about using its litter box until just recently or has done its business outdoors. Suddenly it urinates in the wastebasket or leaves a little heap on the carpet. There may be several reasons for this.

The cat is sick or old. It is thus disturbed in its normal behavior and urgently needs the veterinarian.

Something is wrong with the litter box. Perhaps you haven't cleaned it often enough and the cat can't find any more clean places to squat. Or maybe it's in the wrong place, right next to the feeding bowl, for example. Cats hate to leave their feces where they eat. Or the litter box may be set in a place in the house where someone is always passing by. This also goes against a cat's grain, for cats prefer to be unobserved.

The cat is in love. Males and females spray everywhere to attract partners. After neutering this stops by itself.

The cat is irritated. This is one of the most frequent reasons for lack of cleanliness. Perhaps there are workmen in the house, which has caused confusion and a change of the ordinary environment. Perhaps you've bought new furniture. This at first appears to the cat as endangering its territory. Perhaps a second kitten has arrived and the older inhabitant is trying to show its dominance with visible deposits of feces. In this case, try to strengthen the cat's self-confidence again with much show of affection. At the same time you must clean up the "piddle spot" or the cat will go right back there again. After cleaning with a high-quality soap or vinegar water, for example, cover with a flat piece of plastic wrap and spray with oil of mint or lemon, scents that almost all cats hate. Scolding, yelling, or clapping won't do any good at all and can only disturb your cat even more.

The cat has a behavior disturbance: Determining reasons for uncleanliness is very difficult. If possible, try to keep such a cat where it has much access to the outdoors. That way the chances of its going indoors are somewhat diminished.

Note: Don't use any cleaning agents containing ammonia! These have urine-like scent components, which immediately stimulate the cat to leave its own scent in the just-cleaned spot all over again.

Why the Cat Needs Something to Scratch

There are various reasons why you should offer the cat scratching spots in the form of a tree or a post; otherwise it will use the carpet or a chair for it.

- The cat sharpens its claws. This way it scrapes off the old, worn-out claw surfaces, under which glossy new claws can be seen. Sometimes you find something that looks like a pulled-out claw under the scratching post. But it's only a shed husk of a claw.
- Scratching trains the extending and retracting mechanism of the claws. This is a vital necessity for catching prey, fighting rivals, and climbing.
- Scratching shows superiority. When dominant cats scratch on their posts—or outside, on trees—in the presence of subordinate cats, it's a kind of impressing behavior.
- Scratching is marking. On the underside of the front paws there are actually scent glands, with which the cat rubs on the piece of furniture. Perhaps this is the reason why it keeps seeking out your favorite chair, because it wants to add its own scent to your smell.

My tip: If the cat won't use the scratching post placed at its disposal, no matter what, but keeps attacking your furniture, it may have to do with this scent marking. Attaching a piece of an old wool pullover with your scent on it over the scratching post usually helps.

Neutering—A Necessity?

As usual, this subject is hotly debated. Some are against neutering because they think it only serves the interests of humans, and there are no scientific studies of the consequences for cats.

Feline playmate. The ragdoll is so patient and agreeable by nature that it will even let itself be wheeled around in a doll carriage (see page 127).

Others recommend neutering, and for several reasons:

- Uncontrolled reproduction is prevented.
- Homeless cats roam around, become sick, are shot, run over, or caught and sold for laboratory experiments.
- Cats in heat that live indoors get on others' nerves with their cries, upset, and urine spraying. If they are not mated, they suffer damage to their health.
- Sexually mature tomcats leave scent markings everywhere, even in strange houses, if they can get in and mark over the scent of another cat. During mating they are in particular danger, because they run mindlessly after any female in heat and thus can be run over or involved constantly in battling rivals.

What Happens During Neutering?

The operation is performed under anesthetic by a veterinarian.

For tomcats: the operation (neutering) is not undertaken before the cat reaches sexual maturity, that is at eight to ten months. It involves the surgical removal of the testes with two small incisions.

For female cats: the operation, also called spaying, takes place before the first season of heat (see page 72). This occurs sometime between five and twelve months of age. Of course it's also possible to do it later. The ovaries are removed through an opening in the female's abdominal cavity, usually with a portion of the uterus. Afterward the incision is closed with sutures, which are removed a week later. After the operation the animal normally can be taken home again. Let your cat sleep off the anesthetic in its usual warm spot and take care that she isn't pressured into any climbing forays. Loving attention is ordinarily enough, for as a rule special care isn't required. Usually the cat

Successful animal friendship. A good-natured dog and, most importantly, a well-trained one, can be taught that from now on the kitten belongs to his pack.

Crazy about cats. For dog daddy Roscha, there's nothing nicer than playing with a baby kitten and carrying it around all day long.

owner is more upset than the animal. But of course you should report any complications to the veterinarian. He or she will advise you about anything you need to know.

Sterilization
This word is incorrectly used for the castration of the female cat, for sterilization means merely that the tomcat or female is made sterile by tying off ducts for sperm or ova. The animal thus retains its sex drive, and the uncomfortable side effects in the home are also retained.

The pill: Only recommended for cats intended for breeding that are not supposed to come into heat for the time being. Used over a long period it injures the uterus. There also are newer and safer drugs given by long-acting injections. Ask your veterinarian for advice.

Cats with a Yard

Light, air, and exercise are things that do any creature good. And a cat that is relieved of the constant pursuit of prey because of living with a human being will use the expansion of its living space into the outdoors for excitement and entertainment. Only allow it outside when it is thoroughly at home in the house and make sure that it can get back inside as soon as something frightens it. In the beginning keep it near you and leave something open, for instance the cellar or terrace door. Kitty will very quickly regard the yard as her personal property and chase off any strange cats.

Cat door: One minute the cat sits fussing by the door and wanting to be let out, and the next she's scratching and scraping to be let in again. This happens innumerable times a day, as often as the cat needs to make a round of its territory. This inspection tour is repeated at short intervals, and the cat doesn't like it at all that doors hinder its doing it. So a cat door through which it can leave the house and get back in again is very much to be recommended. The pet store offers various models that are burglar-proof and can be installed in doors and windows.

Securing the yard: Cats with access to the outdoors are subject to more hazards. It's impossible for you to train them not to leave the yard. You can make it more difficult for your cat by securing the fence with electric wire, for example. If the cat receives an uncomfortable shock a couple of times as it climbs over, it will protect itself in the future. But speak with your neighbors about it beforehand!

Neighbors' yards: This is a sad subject that often ends in court and has led to contradictory rulings. One says that a yard owner cannot compel his neighbor to keep his cat indoors just because it hunts birds, occasionally takes a fish out of the pond, and dirties sandboxes, whereas the other proclaims just the opposite. To avoid trouble, which not seldom leads to implacable enmity, you should clear the matter ahead of time (see The Cat and the Law, page 44).

Tattooing the Outdoor Cat
Unfortunately cats are often stolen for experimental laboratories. Therefore you should have a cat that is allowed outdoors tattooed. Ask the veterinarian if this can be done at the time of immunization shots. Under anesthesia an easily read series of numbers (for example, your zip code) is imprinted on the insides of the ears.

In the United States, there is, unfortunately, no central registry that can record identification codes for all pets. There are, however, several commercial registration schemes. The finder of a tattooed cat may have a problem discovering where the cat's owner has registered the number. Hence, your zip code could be the right solution—until you move!

Cat Training—What You Can Achieve with It

The cat living with people can learn some things—if it wants to. It seems to me that instead, my cats have induced me to do certain things to keep them from being led into temptation. This includes never leaving anything edible around uncovered (see Not to steal, page 40).

Five Golden Rules of Training
1. Speak quietly to the cat. Only when it has trust in you will it do what you want.
2. Always forbid the same things. Don't keep it from begging at the table today and then feed it tomorrow.
3. Don't give harsh orders but just utter a firm "No!" when, for example, it scratches the chair again instead of the scratching post.

Opposite page: Careless elegance and grace. This Oriental beauty sits there like a statue. But her expression and sharpened ears indicate tense alertness—what could it be?

4. Always use expressions like "Ugh!" or "No!" or "Down!" or "Out!" Be consistent.

5. Praise and pet the cat when it has obeyed you. Scold it firmly and clearly with words, at most with a light tap with a folded newspaper. Yelling and blows, locking it up, or depriving it of food do no good at all. These things only accomplish the opposite.

What the Cat Should Learn

To know its name: Keep calling it by name while petting, feeding, or other pleasant things. It will very soon know it and come "padding up" when called, especially if there's something good to eat.

Scratching in the right place: Because you certainly don't want the cat to scratch your curtains, rugs, or upholstered furniture, you must provide the appropriate scratching equipment. As soon as the cat begins in a forbidden spot, carry it to the scratching tree or post with a firm "No!," stand it up, and move its paws up and down. Also scratch your own fingernail along the board, for the noise will make the cat curious and want to try it on its own. It depends on your persistence whether the cat finally submits to scratching where you want it to.

Not to sleep on the bed: If you're against an animal sleeping on the bed in principle, you'll have to close the bedroom door. Otherwise the cat will not allow itself to be driven from this comfortable spot.

Not to beg: Not every cat begs, but if it already has this annoying habit, it cannot be entirely broken of begging during mealtimes. It's best if you only feed it at the proper time and, on principle, never feed it from the table.

Not to steal: Not every cat steals. But when one does, it cannot be eradicated completely. Nina looks "disconcerted" when I speak sternly to her, but she doesn't stop pinching food,

"I bash you, you bash me."
These two kitten siblings are still practicing attack and defense as a game. But already their miming and gestures are almost perfect.

40

all the same. Therefore my advice is simply not to leave anything edible lying around and not to leave pots uncovered.

To walk on the lead: Get the kitten used to wearing a harness (see HOW TO: Equipment, page 27) at about three months and let yourself be led by it at first until it also goes where you want it to.

Note: Some cat owners swear by the training provided by a squirt from a water pistol, if the cat insists upon climbing the curtains all the time. It's important that the cat not understand where the uncomfortable dampness comes from.

Cats Must Play

When they play, cats practice all the movements they carry out in hunting. They sneak up, they pounce, they try attacks and defenses, seize prey, follow it, or flee as if they were followed. In their life with humans, hunting is diminished but the capability remains and lies unused if the cat isn't provided with anything to satisfy its drive for this activity. Single cats kept in the house suffer deadly boredom, and you, as the cause of this situation, must undertake to do something about it.

Therefore play with your cat, but of course only if he or she is ready for it. Usually toward evening—because cats become more lively then—it will signal to you in its own way. Mine adore it when I play hide and seek with them, for instance. Our photographer's tomcat loves to roll a glass ball in front of him along the corridor or in the bathtub because it rattles so nicely. Others enjoy themselves with multicolored strands of wool, shiny clumps of aluminum foil, little balls, or fur mice. You have to keep throwing these out for them so that they can chase after them "as in real life."

Young cats at play are practicing hunting techniques for later; thus fishing, for example, is included in their repertoire surprisingly early. In play they throw a ball over the shoulder with a deft movement of a paw, turn around after it with lightning speed, follow it again, and "slay" it. This is the same way an adult cat angles for a fish. She lies in wait until the fish swims near the bank, dips a paw under its body, flips it far behind her onto the grass, and then leaps upon it.

What to Do with the Cat over Vacation?

Leave it home: For this simplest solution you need a responsible person to come in once or twice daily to feed the cat and clean out the litter box and who can spend enough time talking and playing. Ask friends or neighbors to take on this task. In some cities (New York and Los Angeles, for example), there are so-called cat sitters who offer their paid services in the classified advertisements in the newspaper.

Take it with you: You also can accustom your cat to traveling, provided you keep going to the same vacation house. On the other hand, I wouldn't take one with me to a hotel, or camping. You'd have to keep it locked up while you go off to your holiday pleasures. Added to this are the stresses of strange surroundings. In the car you should let the cat out of its carrier only when it can remain quietly in one spot. Watch out when opening windows and doors and keep the cat on a leash at all times. If the journey is longer than six hours, don't give the cat anything to eat the evening before and during the journey so that its digestion is decreased. Have water and a plastic pan of cat litter handy. Remember that you'll need a certificate of immunizations for crossing the border. Get information from your pet store, veterinarian, or the appropriate veterinary department (look in the telephone book).

Boarding: Perhaps you have friends with whom the cat is comfortable. You should look over a cat boarding kennel ahead of time and question the owner in detail. All immunizations will be required there (see page 61). Check with animal shelters, too. Some keep a list of private vacation care places.

How to Get the Cat Through a Move

It's said that cats are more tied to their territory and have a very difficult time coping with a move. However, don't undervalue the relationship the cat has with you, and help it get used to its new territory.

- Keep the animal in a previously emptied room together with its familiar things (basket, litter box) until the confusion of moving is over.
- Drive with it to the new home.
- Put it in an empty room there, again with its things.
- After the house is put in order, lead the cat to the new location of the cat litter box.
- Allow it to explore the new environment quietly and keep talking soothingly to it.
- If the new home has access to the outdoors, gradually accustom the cat to it (see Cats with a Yard, page 37).

Bathing has to happen now and again. When the coat of a Persian is very dirty, you should wash it with water and a special shampoo (see HOW TO: Grooming, pages 46 and 47).

It isn't true that you can't get a cat that has had outdoor access used to a new home without it. It will suffer much more if separated from its people—for instance if the cat is given to the people who take over the old home.

It is true that a cat is sometimes seized with longing for its old territory and returns there. The longest distance that a cat has traveled is supposed to be from Boston to Chicago. How this homing instinct functions is not conclusively explained. Some think that it has to do with the magnetic field of the earth, others believe that the cat, like a migrating bird, makes use of a kind of inner celestial navigation and calculates its path according to the direction of the sun.

My tip: Before you let a cat out in a new place, provide it with a collar with address and telephone number on it (see Tattooing the Outdoor Cat, page 38).

The Old Cat

People say that cats pass a tenth of their lives growing up, a second tenth in age, and the remaining eight tenths they are in their prime, so to speak. Cat lovers who have just acquired a young kitten will have a strong, vital animal to deal with for a long time. Still, I don't want to close the chapter on living with a cat without a look at this last segment of life.

An aging cat need not necessarily decline into bad health. It may perhaps not be so supple in its movements, for instance, it may not climb or jump to its highest spots anymore but may prefer a soft cushion that it can reach comfortably. It will eat less and become thinner, not lick itself so often, and have a rougher coat.

Now you should change its environment as little as possible. The excitement of a young kitten is rather burdensome to it; a move may even be torture.

Care: Even if it exhibits no grave disturbances you should have your older cat examined by the veterinarian every three to four months. It can suffer from constipation, have problems with its teeth, gradually lose its sight and hearing. Be kind to your animal, that's the main thing now.

Putting to sleep: However, if the cat becomes ill and has much pain, you should discuss with your veterinarian whether putting it to sleep isn't the better solution. Only he or she is in the position to administer the lethal injection. The cat will only feel the slight prick of the needle and if you are there holding it in your arms, it will go to sleep very peacefully. If you want to bury your cat in your own yard, you must find out first if that's permitted. In doubtful cases your veterinarian will help you with disposing of its remains.

The Cat and the Law

Community life depends on mutual considerations so that the cat lover living in a rented home in a community setting may expect consideration for his love of animals. On the other hand, the cat keeper also should have consideration for his neighbors and discuss his intentions with the landlord and the neighbors before getting a cat.

Animal protection laws: Although the animal is still often classified by lawmakers as a "thing," some animal protection laws speak of the animal as "fellow creature." No one may cause an animal pain, injury, or harm. Included here is the failure to feed an animal or to feed it enough. Under threat of compensatory fine, one is forbidden to abandon an animal.

Street traffic: Because the animal owner primarily is responsible if a person is killed, injured, or something is damaged because of his animal, he must see to it that his cat doesn't run across the street and thereby endanger drivers or pedestrians. In general, it's advisable to take out an insurance policy for all cats that are allowed to run free.

Dangers to Cats

Here's a list of dangers that shouldn't be overlooked when you live with a cat.

Falling: Secure terraces and open windows with wire or nylon net, because even the most intelligent cat may leap after a fluttering leaf or butterfly and plunge into emptiness.

Being trapped: Don't open and close doors without thinking; secure open tilt windows with special inserts, because the cat wanting to go outside will be caught hanging and strangle itself;

The cat can go in and out whenever it wants through a door flap in a window or door.

artfully carved chairs are a trap, particularly for small kittens, as are cupboards, behind and under which they can crawl.

Suffocating: Plastic bags into which the cat can crawl and get caught should not be left lying around; drawers in which they like to hide and thus can get shut into should not be left open.

Being run over: This danger is basically unavoidable; make running away more difficult by securing the yard (see Cats with a Yard, page 37). In general, neutered cats stay closer to home.

Burning: Place covered pots of water on hot stove burners; turn off irons before leaving the room; do not leave hot plates unsupervised; watch candles, because cats can be alarmed by them and may tip them over; don't leave burning cigarettes and butts lying around.

Wounding: Don't leave lying around needles that the cat may step on or may swallow, or rubber bands; cats can injure themselves dreadfully on barbed wire.

Never leave tablets lying around. Cats may confuse them with vitamin tablets and can be poisoned.

Poisoning: Many plants are poisonous to cats, for instance cyclamen, azalea, dieffenbachia (dumb cane), ivy, lily-of-the-valley, narcissus, carnations, poinsettia, and many more. In general cats are so instinctive that they only nibble on nonpoisonous plants; however, you should find out from your florist or research it in the specialist's literature. Mainly you should keep kittens from access and provide them with a dish of cat grass (see HOW TO: Equipment, page 27). Washing and cleaning materials, chemicals, pills—things that are dangerous for children are also dangerous for kittens. So lock them away!

Hot plates, uncovered pans, and pots with something spluttering and bubbling in them are dangerous for curious cats. They can burn their paws on them.

"Caves," and even better, upholstered with soft laundry, are highly attractive to cats. Not seldom they creep into the washing machine and can be overlooked and caught in the washing.

HOW TO: Grooming

Important Points of Care
Many times a day the cat cleans and licks itself from top to bottom, for cat washing is an extraordinarily thorough affair. Nevertheless, human help is required.

Brushing
Picture 1
Semi-long-haired and short-haired cats need daily coat care only at shedding time, because they cannot then remove all the hair from their coats. Besides, brushing is attention and most cats enjoy it, purring loudly. At first brush from neck to tail with the direction of the fur, then carefully against it, then lightly once again with it to make the fur lie down again.

Washing and Combing
Picture 2 and photographs on pages 42 and 43
Long-haired cats must be bathed if their fur is very dirty. The bath should be big enough so that there is just room enough in it for the cat, for example in the bathroom

2) The fur must be combed carefully out while it is still damp.

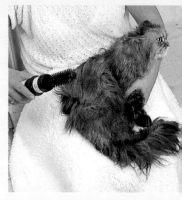

3) You can accustom a Persian to a drier-brush from the time it is very small.

sink. A special shampoo that is also effective against parasites is available at the pet store. Baby shampoo may also be used. Let lukewarm water run into the bowl, hold the cat by the front feet with one hand, and wash with the other. Never put its head under water. Carefully rinse out the shampoo and rub the animal dry with a warmed towel. For combing, take the cat on your lap. With the coarse-toothed metal comb, first thoroughly comb the underhair on the belly and between the legs. Keep talking reassuringly to the cat while you're doing it, and never use force. Then comb with the fine-toothed comb.

1) Most cats enjoy brushing and express it with loud purring.

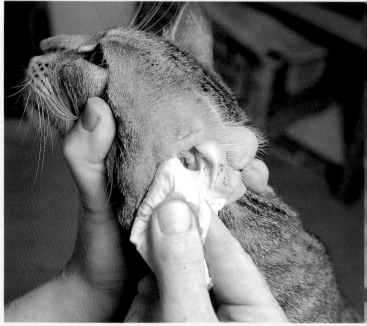

4) Regular examination of the ears is important. Little dark clumps indicate ear mites, which must be treated.

5) Slight incrustations develop in the corners of the eyes now and then; they should be wiped away with a paper tissue.

6) The Persian's coat must be brushed daily.

7) You can clean the Persian's coat with a special powder.

Brushing and Powdering
Pictures 6 and 7

Only brushing brings a shine to the carefully combed hair of the Persian cat. A natural-bristle brush or a special brush with bent-wire bristles is best suited for this. If you hold your Persian cat the way it's done in picture 6, you also can brush the problem areas on the belly and in the chest region. About once a month the coat can be cleaned with a dry shampoo. Use it sparingly, because it dries out the skin. Rub the powder in, let it work overnight, and brush it out thoroughly the next day, also brushing against the direction of the fur.

Removing Knots of Hair
Picture 8

At first divide the snarl into small parts with your fingers and then try to untangle it with the steel comb. If this doesn't work, cut the knot out very carefully.

Important: Unfortunately, many Persians must be sheared under anesthesia by the veterinarian. Animals whose fur is tangled will tear it out in patches, no longer eat, and suffer.

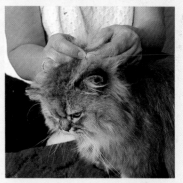

8) Snarls in the fur are separated carefully with the fingers.

Drying
Picture 3

In a warm room the coat can dry by itself. It goes faster with a drier, but this makes the coat dull. A drier-brush is most comfortable for the cat; besides the coat will shine afterwards.

Ear Inspection
Picture 4

Inspect the ears regularly; if necessary, carefully remove dust from the external ear with a tissue. If there are little dark clumps visible, or if the cat scratches frequently and shakes its head, the presence of ear mites is indicated (see Identifying Illnesses, pages 70 and 71).

Eye Cleaning
Picture 5

Slight crusts in the corners of the eyes are removed with a damp, soft paper tissue. Always wipe from outside toward the inside. Persian cats especially need this care daily.

Feeding Your Cat—Correctly and Easily

C ats are predators. Their whole body is adapted to the life-style in the wild. There they live on meat and obtain from their prey—mice, small rodents, also lizards and insects—which they eat entirely, the necessary high concentrations of nutrients from muscles, liver, bones, and organs, including vegetable and mineral matter from the contents of stomachs and intestines. You must adhere to this diet if you want to provide proper and healthy nourishment for your cat as a pet, too.

"The cat never stops mousing," goes an old saying. In its superficial meaning it refers to the fact that the cat doesn't lose its zest for hunting even when it no longer is hungry. In fact, it has even been observed that satisfied cats are better mousers than hungry ones. Thus the hunting drive is not identical with the eating drive. But though well-fed and not excited by the exercise of the hunt, scarcely any cat will overlook a chance to pinch food from the table. This chapter will merely touch on such inappropriate eating habits. Its main concern is with cats' requirements. These determine the stomach's schedule. What must the cat eat in order to grow, to thrive, to have a beautiful coat, clear eyes, and a graceful body? What should you give it to drink, and is feeding with fresh food preferable to ready-made food?

The Cat—A Packet of Energy

"Cats are born mouse-hunters," writes the behavioral researcher Professor Paul Leyhausen. "They can sit for hours at a time with endless patience, that is to say, with true cat patience, in front of a mousehole until the most careful mouse finally peeks out. If Puss were to spring now, the mouse would instantly disappear into the hole again—and for at least several hours. So Puss waits still longer with simply unbelievable patience until the mouse comes completely out of the hole and is a little way away from it—and only then does she pounce."

This all takes energy. So you shouldn't be surprised that a cat who is hungry will polish off its mouse entirely within two minutes at the most.

The energy we're talking about comes from food. The cat finds almost all its necessary nutrients packed in small containers in its prey: meat, bones, organs, including vegetable and mineral materials from the contents of stomach and intestines. The body takes the energy contained in these nutritional building blocks of protein, fat, and carbohydrates and turns it into other energy forms:

- warmth, which keeps the body temperature constantly between 101.3 and 102.2° F (38.5–39° C);

- energy for nervous system function;
- energy for movement, which keeps the muscles and joints going;
- energy for growth, so the body keeps developing new cells.

Snitching cat. The cat likes to snitch from anything she finds on the table, but not because she's particularly crazy about sweets. She just can't stop being curious.

Too Much Food Makes a Cat Fat

As in humans, too much food is turned into fat and stored, which means that cats also can develop spare tires. In the wild this certainly is likely to happen only in years with an abundance of mice. In life with people who offer it food perhaps only in the form of delicacies, it is much more exposed to this danger. In the fall, especially, the cat likes to put on a little fat. So bear in mind when you are feeding your pet as it determinedly begs for a favorite food: Regular overfeeding will make the cat fat.

One-sided Diet Makes a Cat Picky

Even when the cat has been greedily begging for the chicken that you've just taken up and you now give it a little piece, it will carefully sniff and then not eat it. At least not right away.

Three things are to be observed about the eating behavior of domesticated cats:
- Cats are very careful about what they eat.
- Once cats have been spoiled with a favorite food, they will scarcely—or not at all—allow themselves to be switched to another food.

- They actually can become addicted to certain foods, liver, for example.

Therefore avoid a one-sided diet, feed your cat as much variety and as correctly as possible (see Nutrients the Cat Needs, below) and respect the way the cat eats.

Nutrients the Cat Needs

Because your pet no longer needs to provide its own nourishment, it doesn't require so much energy either. Its diet therefore should contain fewer energy-producing nutrients and thus have more protein.

Protein: Cats have a much higher protein requirement than other animal species, five times as much as the dog, for example. Because they can get protein only from animal products, meat is an essential requirement for them. Of course plant protein has an important nutrient value, but not enough for the building material that is vitally necessary to the body. The cat needs protein for growth, for development and renewal of body tissue, and for the production of antibodies, enzymes, and blood. Some examples of foods containing protein are meat, fish, milk, soybeans, oats, and, of course, eggs.

Fat: Fat also contains building blocks that are vitally necessary. Because the cat can't produce these on its own, it must have fat in its diet. Besides energy, fat provides vitamins A, D, E, F, and K. Without them the animal would grow more slowly, be very susceptible to illness, and usually be sterile. On the other hand, too much fat isn't good, for what doesn't get used is stored in immense fat deposits. Besides being in meat, fat is contained in butter and oils of sunflower, corn, and wheat germ.

Carbohydrates: These are converted directly into energy by the cat's body and partly stored in the liver and muscles for "time of need." These important energy stores are contained in rice, potatoes, oat flakes, or vegetables; however, they must be cooked and mixed with the food in small amounts. Too much carbohydrate will be turned into fat and make the cat overweight. Cellulose, carbohydrate contained in plant fiber, cannot be digested by cats at all; but it serves as useful bulk material and regulates the bowel (see Cat Grass, page 27).

Vitamins and minerals: In a well-balanced diet they should be available to cats in sufficient quantity. Too much is just as harmful as too little. You would do well to mix in vitamin and mineral preparations (available from the pet store) with a growing kitten's food.

Prepared Food

Ready-made food in boxes, bags, or cans is practical. You need only open a can and find a menu that is constituted to offer the cat everything it needs. At least that's what the manufacturer

Tasty little tidbit. Cats don't like to take food out of your hand, the way the dog does, for instance. They prefer to lick a proffered finger clean, which corresponds more to their way of eating.

promises; moreover, the law requires them to give the precise composition of the food on the label.

These days, however, it's not just the matter of composition but also the quality of the products from which the food is produced. Responsible manufacturers of course make sure that only the best quality ingredients are used, but unfortunately there are some manufacturers who are not so punctilious. Thus a "consumer's critical eye" is necessary. Another consideration is whether your cat tolerates or likes the food. This can vary from brand to brand. What tastes good to one cat may even make another one vomit. Thus you, as a responsible cat owner, are asked to make the tough choice among the different offerings. Prepared food is available in different forms:

Moist food is complete food in cans and consists of a mixture of muscle meat, organs, or different ocean fish, to which plant proteins, grains, minerals, and vitamins have been added.

My tip: Because of the soft consistency of the food, the cat's teeth and gums are not polished enough and this can lead to a buildup of tartar and to gum disease. Therefore change off with freshly prepared food and now and then also give veal gristle.

Dried food is a highly concentrated complete diet from which up to about 10 percent of the water has been removed. Cats need to eat very little of it to meet their food requirement, but they must drink that much more. Observe how much the cat drinks of the water you give it. As a rule of thumb, for every 3 ½ ounces (100 g) of dried food, 3 ⅓ fluid ounces (100 cc) of water. Often the amount of water is not enough to make up for the body's overall loss of it. Neutered tomcats, especially, which have a tendency toward bladder stones and life-threatening urinary blockages, will suffer from this and may become seriously ill.

My tip: Give this crunchy food only sparingly as an extra so that the cat has something hard for its teeth to gnaw on now and again.

Sitting up and begging is a rarity in cats. Tomcat Robin sometimes gets up on his hind legs for a tasty bite.

Fresh Food—The Old and New Alternative

Really it's very old hat, for there always have been people who preferred to offer their cats home-cooked meals. After you've read what you need to take into consideration in feeding your cat, you really can't go wrong. Try sometime to see if your cat likes the menus suggested in HOW TO: Feeding, pages 56 and 57. They go down very well with my cats.

You must bear several things in mind when you prepare the individual foods, however:

Meat: Best used lean and without bones. Suitable are the muscle meat of beef, veal, lamb, rabbit, game; poultry smells better cooked. Also pork must be cooked because here there is a danger of transmission of disease, such as the always fatal pseudorabies or toxoplasmosis. Any raw meat can transmit parasites or salmonella.

Farm cats. They live in stables and barns and all outdoors. They like to sit in high places and observe their surroundings. Moreover they prefer to seek out sun-warmed corners and niches in which they are protected on at least two sides.

Organ meats: Always cook heart (without fat), lean udder, and kidney; wash kidney well beforehand. Liver can be fed raw or cooked; raw has a laxative effect, cooked is constipating. Don't use it exclusively because it can lead to vitamin A poisoning, which results in bone deformities and crippling, among other things.

Fish: Don't feed raw, especially freshwater fish, but lightly steamed and boned. Only give about once a week, because otherwise cats smell of it too much.

Eggs: Only the yolk raw and once a week. White must be cooked, because raw it eliminates the vitamin biotin, which is an important one for cats. Traditionally, yolks have been given raw, but note that raw eggs have been found to carry salmonella.

Fat: Easily digested fats like oils of corn germ, wheat germ, or sunflower mixed with food.

Bones: For gnawing on to prevent development of tartar. Only small veal bones or gristle. No chicken bones, because these splinter and can become embedded in the mouth.

What else is important in preparation of fresh food:
- Use only items that you also would use for yourself. The more natural the food is, the more vitality its essential ingredients will probably still have too.

Farm cats have to provide their own food. So that they will be diligent mousers, the farm wife gives them a saucer of fresh milk only once a day.

The wrong food makes the cat sick. Basic nutrients are protein, fat, and carbohydrate, and vitamins and minerals. They must be in proper balance with each other and be fed in amounts that are sufficient but not too large. Too much food makes a cat fat, and unvaried diet makes it choosy.

- Provide as varied a diet as possible, for instance in the mornings a good quality prepared food, in the evening home-made fresh food.
- You can cook ahead, but remember that food in the refrigerator keeps fresh for four days at the most.
- If you want to freeze the food, pack it in the appropriate-sized portions.
- It's possible that your cat will reject the new food at first. In that case, start with smaller portions and slowly increase them until you are up to the cat's required food quantities. Otherwise give it much time and patience and always make sure there is a dish of water. If you are dealing with a particularly hardheaded cat, it may be that you'll have to return to the old way of feeding.

Drinks and Drinking Habits

Water is the proper drink for cats. Some get their entire water requirement from their food. The largest part of it is contained there in any case, but still you always should offer them a saucer with fresh water in it so they can quench their thirst according to need and mood. The reason cats get along with so little water is that as former prairie and savannah dwellers they can retain far more water in their kidneys than most other animals. However, they need water to live and if they are ever denied food, they are more likely to die of dehydration than starvation. Sometimes you can observe that cats will make use of any possible water source. They lap at puddles, lean into watering cans, or lick from the bathroom floor. A favorite trick is to hang directly under the water faucet, as my Nina does. She ordinarily only does it at the sink in the bathroom, although I am much more often at the kitchen faucet.

Milk is not a drink but a food for cats. It contains many nutrients, for example protein and calcium, and should therefore be offered to all pregnant cats and to little kittens. For these it must be rich in fat and not skimmed at all or thinned with water, for cat's milk is much fatter than cow's milk. You can add one-third water to canned milk. But cow's milk contains more milk sugar than the milk of the mother cat and even the protein is different, so many cats cannot tolerate milk and get diarrhea from it. You then mustn't give it to them anymore. Fundamentally, however, milk is not appropriate for quenching thirst or maintaining the water balance.

Ten Cat Eating Habits

1. Cats can get used to a set time. They adapt to it and come running from afar. You keep to it too and always feed them at the same time.

2. Cats like it fresh. Give them a new portion at each mealtime and if they haven't eaten it all, measure it and give them that much less the next time. Don't fill their plate.

3. Cats like their food at room temperature. Therefore never feed directly from the refrigerator.

4. Cats quickly become spoiled over food and therefore possibly too fat if you only feed them treats. Provide variety and variation in the meals. For dieting, don't make the cat fast but measure out smaller portions.

5. Cats can beg at the dinner table with a persistence that would soften a stone. Don't let yourself be taken in.

6. Cats like all the things that people eat, particularly if they can be pilfered from the table. You should break your cat of this bad habit (see page 40). Otherwise, some leftovers from your own meal won't hurt now and again, but they shouldn't be too sharply seasoned, too salty, or too sweet.

7. Cats like things clean. Their feeding bowl should be washed out at each meal, but only with hot water. Don't use any cleaning materials!

8. If cats go outside, they also should have something to eat and drink provided. They don't always catch enough mice to be full.

9. Cats need four times as much protein as dogs; therefore dog food is not suitable for the long term.

10. Cats are predators and need animal protein. They will suffer metabolic disturbances if you try to make vegetarians out of them.

Opposite page: Persian cat in the sunlight. In bright light the pupils narrow to small slits, so that the amber eyes shine out of the black fur like Chinese lanterns.

How and What the Cat Eats
On these pages you will find a few typical eating habits of the cat with practical directions for preparing simple cat menus.

Drinking
Picture 1
The cat can shape its long, flexible tongue like a spoon. With it she ladles the water into her mouth.

Eating
Picture 2
Cats are deliberate eaters. They hold their heads slanted to one side as they eat, making it look as though eating were something unseemly. Morsel by morsel they drag the food out of the dish, lay it carefully next to it, sniff it thoroughly, and only then eat it.

Eating in a Group
Picture 3
Cats that have free run outdoors, especially, don't mind gathering around a common eating dish. A certain order of dominance will be observed, though. Thus the top cat will begin. If the cat society is peaceful, each one will get its food, even the lowest on the totem pole, though it must wait for a while.

Crouching in front of the Bowl
Picture 4
The typical eating posture for a cat is the crouch. Front legs and hind legs are bent, the rear end is slightly raised, the tail tidily coiled around the body.

56

1) In drinking, the tongue is used like a ladle.

2) The cat takes its food out of the dish piece by piece.

Cleaning
Picture 5
When the cat has eaten, first it thoroughly licks its mouth. Not satisfied with that, then it dampens its paw with its tongue a number of times and uses it to "wash" its cheeks clean.

How Much the Cat Eats
The normal body weight of the cat ranges between 7¾ and 11 pounds (3.5–5 kg). It needs about 4½ to 8¾ ounces (125–250 g) of complete diet per day. Some cats can eat even more without becoming fat. Tomcats need more than females; neutered cats shouldn't eat so much, for they tend to put on weight. A pregnant cat should not be given more but should have more nourishing food, preferably divided into four or five portions throughout the day. Nursing cats consume more food, however, specifically about 16 ounces (450 g), divided into several portions.

Practical Preparation Tips
- Raw meat is the most natural food for cats. It must be fresh and be from irreproachable sources; otherwise there is danger of disease (see Fresh Food—The Old and New Alternative, page 51). Any meat from pigs should only be served cooked!
- The cat needs nourishing food but not necessarily tasty, as we understand it. This means hands off salt and other seasonings.
- For a supply of vitamin A, the cat needs 4 to 5 ounces (100–150 g) of liver per week. Apportion it ahead of time, keep it in the freezer, and daily mix a portion into the food.
- Chicken necks and chicken giblets should not be bought deep frozen if possible, because there can be danger of salmonella during thawing.
- A teaspoonful of olive oil or margarine in the food once a week ensures that the cat will not vomit up hairballs it has swallowed but will excrete them.
- If you convert the amounts of weights in the following recipes into cup measures you'll have less work.

3) Cats who live outdoors gladly gather around a common eating dish.

4) Cats often assume this crouching position when eating.

Simple Recipes for Cat Menus
The quantities given make enough food for one day.

Meat Dish
5 oz (150 g) raw meat—beef, mutton, rabbit, game, minced into cat-sized morsels
2 Tbs 6-grain baby gruel
1 tsp yeast-vitamin flakes

2 Tbs pureed carrots
1 Tbs liver

Fish Dish
5 oz (150 g) frozen fish, slightly steamed in water
1 Tbs cooked rice
1 tsp oil or margarine
2 Tbs cooked vegetables
1 tsp yeast flakes

Poultry Dish
5 oz (150 g) cooked chicken, cut into cat-sized morsels
2 Tbs flaked mild hard cheese
1 Tbs cottage cheese
1 tsp corn oil
2 Tbs pureed carrots
1 tsp yeast-vitamin flakes
1 Tbs liver

Organ Meat Dish
5 oz (150 g) turkey or beef heart, roasted and cut into cat-sized morsels
2 Tbs cooked vegetables
2 Tbs flaked mild hard cheese

5) The cat washes its face after eating.

1 tsp corn oil
1 Tbs liver
1 tsp yeast-vitamin flakes
1 Tbs cottage cheese

Note: These recipes are developed through my own experience. Because every cat responds differently, try them out to see whether your cat tolerates them too.

57

What to Do If Your Cat Is Sick

Many cat owners can confirm that a cat laid low after a fight with a torn ear, a bite wound to the bone, or a great hole in its fur may be on its feet again astonishingly soon. As a rule, sick and injured cats recover very quickly and it can be said that in general cats are by nature robust, tough, hardy, and more resistant to illness than other animals. Indeed, there are cat owners who don't know what a sick cat is. You can be one of these too. Make it your goal to keep your cat well. You can do this if you feed it properly, groom it well, maintain it correctly, and handle it lovingly.

If your cat ever does get sick, don't hesitate to take it to the veterinarian. His or her advice and treatment and your appropriate care will soon get your cat up and around again.

Prevention Is Better Than Cure

You can do a lot to keep your cat from ever becoming sick. Besides providing the right living conditions, you should not fail to undertake a few necessary preventive measures. If Puss doesn't suffer anything else untoward, she can live for 14 years and longer.

You should know that: A healthy cat is lively, curious, playful, and from an early age cleans itself regularly and thoroughly.

Other signs of good health are:
- a thick, shining coat,
- clear eyes,
- clean ears (also inside),
- undamaged teeth without deposits,
- a pink tongue with no bad odor,
- a soft, dark formed stool,
- yellow, clear urine.

On the other hand, a sick cat sits around listlessly, doesn't eat, and may be scratching constantly. Further signs that indicate a health problem or illness can be found on pages 70 and 71.

Inoculations, the Best Precaution

Inoculations are the first line of imperative precautionary measures. A cat that isn't inoculated can contract infectious diseases that usually are fatal.

A further prevention is worming, which must be undertaken regularly for all cats that go outdoors.

Shots: As long as the kitten is nursing (eight to ten weeks), it is protected from illness through the mother's milk. After this, it must be immunized for the first time. To receive shots, the animal

Kitten is sick. Now it primarily needs much sleep and proper care so that it will be well again soon.

Double spread on previous pages: Sunrise is quitting time for the cat. After she's roamed about all night long, she heads purposefully home to a filled dish and a well-deserved rest.

must be healthy and free of parasites. Before getting the cat's shots, take a stool sample to the veterinarian, for only he can administer the shots. He records it on an inoculation certificate and at the same time notes which shots will need to be repeated when. Keeping to that schedule is important!

Note: Shots are required for traveling abroad. Because the regulations vary from country to country, you should find out about it far enough ahead of time (veterinarian, veterinary bureau).

Inoculations are necessary for

- Feline distemper. This very infectious viral disease is not only carried from animal to animal but also by secondary carriers, such as hands or shoes.
- Rabies. It is contagious to humans. Cats that go outdoors always must be immunized.
- "Cat flu." A lingering infectious illness that is now spread worldwide. It is transmitted from one animal to another, for instance through urine or saliva. Diagnosed through the so-called ELISA test, which often is required of stud cat owners.
- Infectious pneumonitis. This term includes several infectious respiratory diseases. The shot only immunizes against specific pathogens and thus is very narrow in its effect. Proof is required by most cat boarding kennels.

Important: The shot is only effective one or two weeks after it is administered, at the earliest. You should take this into consideration, for example, when you are planning a trip.

Diseases for Which There Is No Immunization

- Feline infectious peritonitis (FIP). This chronic feline disease, which produces increasing accumulation of fluid in the abdomen or the chest, is always fatal.

Immunization Table

	Distemper	Pneumonitis	Rabies	"Cat Flu"
First shot may be given at	7–8 wks	7–8 wks	from 12 wks	9 wks
Boosters for kittens under 12 wks	after 3–4 wks	after 3–4 wks		1. after 3–4 wks 2. after 1 yr
Boosters for kittens over 12 wks old or older cats	after 1 yr	after 2–4 wks	after 1 yr	1. after 3–4 wks 2. after 1 yr
Boosters for maintaining immunization	every 2 yrs	yearly	yearly	yearly

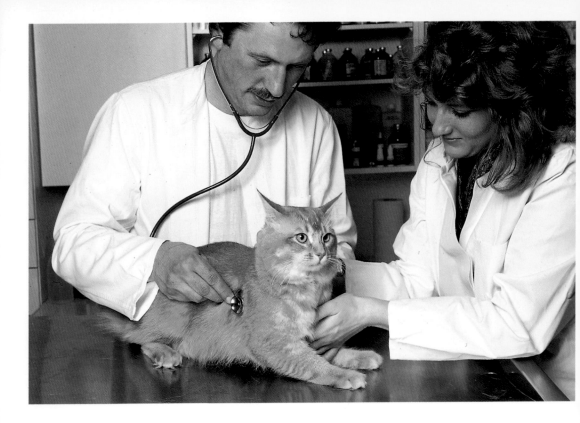

Visit to the veterinarian. This strange, threateningly smelling place makes the cat anxious. The only help is loving talk and an exam-ination that is carried out expertly and speedily.

• Pseudorabies (Aujeszky's disease). This virus disease, which occurs predominantly in swine, is transmitted to cats through pork and is incurable. Therefore only cooked pork should be fed to cats. By the way, people are not infected by this disease!

A word about "cat AIDS"

Although the feline immunodeficiency virus (FIV) does belong to the same virus group as the cause of AIDS in humans, it has nevertheless been established that it is not threatening to humans. Therefore you need have no anxiety and also need not part with your cat if it should be determined that it has FIV. Let the veterinarian advise you what to do for your cat.

Worming

Young kittens usually don't have worms if their mothers are free of them. But the veterinarian can only determine this for sure if you bring him a stool sample when you come for shots. If necessary, he will then prescribe a worm treatment (preparation in paste or tablet form).

Cats that run free keep getting worms, be it through other cats, mice, fleas, or lice from the ground or water. These cats should be wormed regularly every three to six months.

Indoor Cats can get worms by being given raw pork or fish. Use these foods cooked only!

Note: It's extremely important to follow the veterinarian's instructions exactly when administering the worm cure!

Diseases That Are Communicable to Humans

There are a number of disease-causing organisms that can infect both humans and cats, but you mustn't let this idea disturb you unduly. An indoor cat that is immunized and eats only cooked or canned food rarely catches anything that could be dangerous to you too. Even with an outdoor cat, which can come into contact with more germs and parasites, you needn't fear infection as long as you observe the necessary precautions and follow the hygienic rules. These should be a matter of course in any dealings with animals anyway.

Recently I was called by a friend who is expecting a baby. She asked me if she really had to give away her cat. Her mother and mother-in-law were nagging at her and finally she also was beginning to be afraid that her Lizzie could infect her and the baby. I asked her what the doctor had told her. He routinely had examined her for toxoplasmosis, had found nothing, and only recommended that for the duration of her pregnancy she not have too close body contact with Lizzie and to let someone else clean the litter box.

What I mean to say with this is that you should get the advice of experts and out of love for your cat not let yourself be led astray by well-meaning advice. Always go to the veterinarian immediately when your cat shows symptoms of illness. And in case of doubt about yourself, always go to your doctor and be sure to tell him you have a cat. It is cruel and shows ignorance to give an animal to a shelter or, even worse, simply abandon it because of fear of infection.

Basically the following diseases and parasites can be transmitted to humans:

Rabies: Any cat that is allowed outdoors must be immunized against it (see page 61).

Toxoplasmosis: It is primarily dangerous to women who are pregnant, because it can cause serious damage to the brain and eyes of the fetus. Women therefore should seek advice from their doctor at the very beginning of pregnancy about keeping a cat and have their blood checked for toxoplasmosis twice at intervals of six weeks.

Microsporia: It is caused by a skin fungus and manifests itself in falling hair and scratching. Treatment by the veterinarian. To prevent reinfection, keep disinfecting sleeping basket, comb, brush, toys, and anything else the cat comes into contact with. Sometimes the things must be disposed of entirely.

Intestinal worms: Regular worming prevents these.

Fleas, mites, ticks: Put a flea collar on your cat. It protects against infestation. But be careful with cats that run loose. They can be hung up by it and strangle. To diminish this danger, have the pet store show you how to fasten the collar properly. The animals can be treated with flea powder or shampoo (ask at the druggist or let your veterinarian prescribe). When fleas appear, thoroughly vacuum cracks and crevices, especially under rugs

Examining the ears. If the cat is scratching often and constantly shaking its head, it indicates ear mites.

and carpets; fleas can survive there for up to four months. When mites appear, thoroughly disinfect all places where cats lie (basket, sofa, and other places).

If you have found a tick on your cat, grasp it with tick tweezers and twist it out of the skin counterclockwise. You also can put a dot of oil or benzene on it, and when the tick lets go, carefully pull it out with tweezers. The head should not remain in the flesh or the spot will become inflamed.

The Visit to the Veterinarian

Because of the need for shots, you'll be going to the veterinarian at least once a year. Thus it's obvious that you want to find a specialist who understands something about cats and in whom you can have confidence. Talking with other cat owners and asking at the pet store or at the cat breeder's society will help make the choice easier for you.

Transport: Don't simply carry your cat in your arms when you go but place it in a cat carrier (see Glossary, page 102) and don't let the cat loose in the waiting room. Don't forget to keep on talking reassuringly to it.

Consultation: Give the veterinarian a brief but exact report of the symptoms. It's best if you make a list beforehand. Answer his questions clearly so that he can find out what he needs to know. Perhaps he won't be able to make a diagnosis right away but must do some additional tests, for instance on blood and stool.

You should prepare yourself ahead of time for these questions:

- How is your cat eating?
- Has it vomited, had diarrhea or constipation (perhaps bring a stool sample with you)?
- Is it drinking more than usual?
- Is it vomiting more than usual?
- Have you taken its temperature and found fever, and if so, how high was it?
- Has it been scratching a lot, for instance at its ears, and does it keep shaking its head?
- Has the cat fallen, has it gotten caught or pinched, or has there been any other accident?
- Has it been coughing with its neck outstretched?
- Has it lost a lot of weight?

If the veterinarian prescribes medication, you should adhere precisely to the dosage and length of treatment and keep on giving the medication even if it seems to you that the illness is cured. You also should follow all the veterinarian's other instructions exactly.

The Cat as Patient

As long as the cat is so sick that it's too weak to stand on its feet, you'll have a relatively easy time with taking care of it. But then

The cat has nine lives, it's said, and actually there's a good deal of truth in this. The cat's ability to get out of tight situations and to appear hale and healthy again is often amazing. You shouldn't rely on this, however, but give the cat the right kind of life. This includes the right diet and loving attention, so that the cat feels good and can live to be twelve to fifteen years old.

Opposite page: Both of these young Siberian cats from the far North also love a sunny place in the garden.

you'll have to resort to all kinds of tricks. The cat is not a docile patient, and it will not realize that everything is being done in its own interest.

Sickbed: A shallow carton or basket with a somewhat raised edge so that the cat can't fall out; furnish it with a soft cushion covered with a washable cover that can be changed.

Location: In a warm, draft-free place where you comfortably can take care of the patient. If there are other cats around, they should be isolated from the sick one if the illness is infectious.

Feeding: If the cat refuses even its favorite food, use a hypodermic (without needle!) to slowly shoot unsalted meat or chicken broth into the side of its mouth behind the eyeteeth. Don't inject a flood or the cat will choke.

Drinking: The sick animal must take in fluid at all costs or it will become dehydrated. So if it won't drink by itself, you must squirt water in with the hypodermic.

Pills: A cat may allow itself to be duped once, but then it will see through the whole thing, especially if it hears the rattle of the pill bottle. Try the following: For giving pills, settle the cat on your lap so that his face is turned away from you. Hold the pill ready between the thumb and pointer finger of one hand. With the other hand, gently but firmly grasp the head of the animal behind the teeth. He involuntarily will open his mouth. Now shove the pill into his jaws as far back as possible, hold the jaws shut, and massage the throat downwards with the other hand until the pill is swallowed without a trace.

Drops: If dripped on its paws, the cat will lick off the drops as quickly as possible by itself, provided they taste good to it. Bitter medicines can be instilled the way I've described for food (see above).

Taking temperature: It is easier if you have someone to help. While holding the cat at the front and talking reassuringly to it, lift the tail slightly and carefully introduce the thermometer, which has been greased with Nivea cream, about ¾ inch (2 cm) into the anus and leave it there for one to two minutes. The temperature of a healthy cat ranges from about 101.3 to 102.2° F (38.5–39° C).

Feeling the pulse: The pulse is best felt inside the thigh, and of course so that the cat isn't even conscious of it. Stroke the cat with one hand and feel with the other until you feel the beat of the pulse. The pulse beat of a cat is normally between 110 and 140 per minute.

Eye and ear drops: To instill drops in the eye with the special dropper bottle, hold the cat's head firmly from behind and at the same time carefully draw back the cat's eyelid with the index finger. Be careful never to allow the tip of the dropper to touch the eyeball!

When putting drops in the ears, carefully pull back the ear and thus open the ear canal. Afterwards gently massage the ear at the base so that the fluid will be distributed along the aural canal.

Shots: A cat suffering from diabetes must receive an injection daily. Have the veterinarian show you the right way to hold it.

The body of a cat should be soft and supple, the skin must fit loosely, so to speak, and the belly should not feel hard and tight.

When you are experienced, the cat scarcely will feel it. A friend even told me that her cat regularly presented the "shot spot" at the appointed time.

First Aid for Simple Health Problems

As an animal keeper you are responsible for seeing that your ailing cat is provided with quick and appropriate help. When in doubt, always turn to the veterinarian. But there are one or two things you can do yourself too. All the natural remedies mentioned can be obtained from the drugstore.

Treatment for simple diarrhea (brothy stool; when vomiting also present, go to veterinarian at once): If caused by wrong diet (milk, raw liver, fish that's gone bad), discontinue diet immediately. Introduce chamomile or peppermint tea (with hypodermic without needle, see page 66). Mash some dried billberries (available in health-food stores) in a mortar and add to tea. If no improvement after two days, go to the veterinarian.

Treatment for simple constipation (difficulty in evacuating stool): Purebred cats (long hairs) can suffer from this. Offer some milk as a laxative frequently or 1 teaspoon of olive oil in the food once or twice. Improvement should appear after two days. If vomiting occurs in conjunction with constipation, get the advice of the veterinarian.

Treatment for sniffles: Try a chamomile steam bath in which you sit in front of the kettle under a towel with the animal on your lap. If there is no improvement, go to the veterinarian.

Treatment for coughing: A steam bath also will help for coughing, namely of equal parts of coltsfoot, marshmallow, and chamomile. If no improvement, go to your veterinarian.

Treatment for eye inflammations: For swollen conjunctiva carefully treat with drops of an antibiotic ointment usually combined with a drug to reduce the soreness. If no improvement within three days, go to the veterinarian.

Treatment for bruises: This can occur when a cat leaps. Treat with continually replaced poultices of tincture of Arnica or calendula (dilute properly). Get the advice of a veterinarian.

Treatment for superficial wounds: Treat with a bandage of calendula tincture or salve or tincture of chamomile. Deeper wounds (porcupine quills, dog bites) should be left to the care of a veterinarian.

Treatment for shock after an accident: One of the most important lifesaving first aid measures. Place the cat on its right side (naturally only if it has no external wounds there) on a blanket or towel by carefully lifting while supporting the neck and the rump from behind. Wrap the cover around it and bed the animal comfortably in a basket or on your lap. Hold the head somewhat lower than the rest of the body so that the brain will remain perfused with blood. Thus carry it to the veterinarian, whom you should have informed of the accident ahead of time.

Cats that have been toasting themselves on the heating unit and then make an inspection tour of the yard immediately afterward can get a cough relatively easily, but it isn't threatening.

Health Checkup

Cats have the reputation for being tough, hardened, and more resistant to illness than are most other animals. You can contribute to the maintenance of this natural resistance by performing the examination procedures described below from time to time.

But don't forget that the most effective way to keep your cat healthy is proper daily care. For the animal this means that it can live exactly the way its species is supposed to. That is, sleeping or resting most of the day without being disturbed; in its periods of wakefulness, using all the capabilities of its body and mind so that it feels itself unrestrained. To be nourished sufficiently, i.e., with the nutrients that it might find in a mouse, for example, and that is an astonishingly varied menu (see Feeding Your Cat—Correctly and Easily, page 48).

- Check to see if the territory—apartment, house, yard—is set up so that the cat can go about its affairs: sleeping, resting, observing, climbing, scratching, hunting, playing, and all the rest.
- See to it that the cat's cleanliness requirements are met: keep litter box clean, wash feed bowls, clean ears, brush coat.
- Remove any hazards for the cat as well as possible (see Dangers to Cats, page 44).
- Give your cat nutritious food and make sure it's fresh and in the right quantities (see HOW TO: Feeding, pages 56 and 57).

Teeth Examination
Picture 1
About three weeks after birth the kitten gets its milk teeth, which are replaced by the permanent teeth at about the fifth month of life. The change of teeth proceeds almost unmarked; the milk teeth are either spit out or swallowed. The set of milk teeth has 26, the permanent set has 30

teeth. In your inspection, observe for the following:

Tartar buildup: In cats, it's produced by food that is too soft and drinking water that is too hard. You can prevent it by giving your cat a small veal bone or veal gristle to gnaw on once a week and giving it boiled water to drink. If tartar has developed, it must be chipped off by the veterinarian.

Gum inflammation: This often arises from tartar or from infections in the mouth and jaws. It is recognized by a red line along the gums. Besides, the cat's mouth smells bad.

Anal Examination
Picture 2
Fecal material stuck around the anus indicates diarrhea. It can have a number of causes, for instance, digestive upset because of diet, parasites in the intestine, infection, or virus disease. Thus diarrhea is always an alarm signal of the body, especially when it continues for a long time, and must be carefully observed. You can remedy a simple diarrhea with a healing treatment (see page 67).

Skin Examination
Picture 3
Skin diseases can develop very quickly in cats. For this reason you should examine the skin regularly to nip in the bud any possible disease. This is also important for you, for many skin diseases are communicable to humans (see page 63). Therefore you should take the cat to the veterinarian early on.

Clear indication that something is not right with the skin

1) Tartar should be removed regularly because it can lead to gum inflammation.

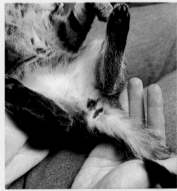

2) Fecal matter clinging to anus and sexual area indicates diarrhea.

3) Reddened areas on the skin or crusty circles indicate skin infections, which may have various causes.

Ear Examination
Picture 4

Cats' ears can be infested with ear mites internally or have skin disease externally or be inflamed. Diseases of this sort can be caught at the beginning through regular examination and treated immediately so that they don't worsen. If the cat shakes its head all the time, keeps scratching at its ears, and is clearly irritated, you should examine the ears. If you discover a smeary deposit and brown encrustation in and around the ear, ear mites are indicated. Very reddened or inflamed skin in the entry to the ear (shine a flashlight in) is a sign of ear inflammation. It can, if not treated promptly, lead to a dangerous middle ear infection. Small bare spots on the ear indicate a skin disease.

Eye Examination
Picture 5

The eyes of a cat are normally clear and clean. With conjunctivitis, on the other hand, they are red and sensitive to pressure, they exude a gooey yellow discharge, and the nictitating membrane is visible (Treatment for eye inflammations, see page 67). Sometimes foreign bodies get into the eyes, such as a grass seed, little hair, or sand grain. The indication for this is a sudden, abundant flow of tears in one eye. If the foreign body has become embedded in the eye surface, it causes severe pain. Even if you can see it, you should have it removed only by the veterinarian.

is constant scratching in the same spot.

Fungus diseases, microsporia for example, are recognizable as round, hairless places that sometimes display strong crust or scale development. Parasites such as fleas can be seen by inflamed spots and falling hair. But your cat also can suffer from allergies or hormone disturbances. All these diseases can only be recognized properly and treated appropriately by your veterinarian.

4) Smeary deposits or reddened skin are a sign of ear diseases.

5) Foreign bodies in the eyes are painful and must be removed by the veterinarian.

Gentle therapist. By their natures cats can be very reassuring for old people, and they radiate infinite tranquility.

Identifying Illnesses

Symptom	Possible Cause, Which You May Try to Remedy Yourself
Sits around listlessly	Boredom, no stimulation to play
Doesn't eat	Dislikes food provided
Vomiting	Eating grass, swallowed hair while licking, eating too fast, or food too cold
Drooling	Great excitement
Foul mouth odor	Directly attributable to food, for instance fish
Constant thirst	Strongly seasoned leftovers
Diarrhea	Wrong diet (milk, raw liver, fish gone bad)
Eats more than usual	Recouping after a few days of straying or after giving birth
Straining without expression of stool or urine	Problems with elimination because of lack of exercise or wrong diet
Running eyes	Conjunctivitis from draft or strong cleaning materials
Sneezing	Irritation of nasal mucus membrane, allergy
Coughing	Choking
Accelerated breathing	Panting in great heat, shock, anxiety, or stress
Scratching	Licking and cleaning coat
Appearance of nictitating membrane, when third eyelid partly covers eye	Frequent appearance suggests poor health; occasional swelling through injury to eye in fight
Head shaking and/or carrying head at an angle	Ear inflammation
Bleeding	Small wounds in skin

Alarm Signal When These Symptoms Also Are Present	Possible Diagnosis; Requires Immediate Treatment by Veterinarian
Frequent vomiting or diarrhea more than 24 hrs, difficulty breathing, circulatory collapse	Uncertain; virus infection, poisoning, bacterial infection
Vomiting or diarrhea	Everything possible
Apathy, diarrhea	Worms, poisoning (for example, from plants), virus infection, bacterial infection
Hardly eats anything	Dental tartar, gum inflammation
Vomiting, trembling, drooling	Infection of oral cavity, gum disease, stomach upset, vitamin B deficiency
Weight loss, vomiting	Kidney or liver disease, diabetes
Bloody stool, vomiting	Virus infection, worms, bacterial infection
Clay-colored stool, rough fur, weight loss	Worms, pancreatic disease
Cries of pain	Constipation, rectal blockage, bladder and urethral inflammation
Discharge of pus	Purulent conjunctivitis, eye injury, feline pneumonitis
Fever, difficulty breathing, coughing	Cold, virus infection
Spitting mucus, fever, difficulty breathing	Cold, bronchitis, virus infection, foreign body in throat
Fever, coughing	Respiratory infection, chest or lung injury
Constantly scratching all over body	Ear mites, fleas, lice, skin inflammation
Eye discharge	Wound, infection, foreign body in eye, tumor
Scratching behind the ear only, pain	Ear mites, middle ear inflammation
Blood from mouth, anal region, large wounds	Infection of intestine, uterus, and bladder, battle wounds, accident

Housebroken. At about three weeks of age, little kittens begin to use the litter box. They learn it through imitation, for the mother no longer concerns herself with their cleanliness. Now you have to watch out for digestive disturbances.

Cat Love—A Story With a Sequel

Two to three times a year a female cat comes into season. She can have kittens just as often. Birth control is therefore necessary, for the human also bears the responsibility for seeing that the kittens are well maintained. If you want to have the first-hand experience of your cat having kittens, you will find interesting information about it in this chapter. In all the delight over the thought of sweet little kittens, however, you mustn't forget that raising kittens isn't something to be done with one hand tied.

Meow-Meow, our first cat, ought to have kittens, it was decided in family council. Because we went to the country every weekend, we knew that there was a splendid red tomcat there who already had registered his interest in our cat. The "arranged marriage" worked out fabulously, which is not necessarily always the case with cats (see Foreplay—A Rigorous Ritual, page 73). When Meow-Meow began to show the first signs of pregnancy, we were pleased enormously. For at that time I believed that my cats must have young at least once in their lives.

Nevertheless, experts agree that raising kittens does not alter the behavior of a female cat. She becomes neither more devoted nor more social, which is to say, the character and personality of the cat remain the same whether she has kittens or not. Basically, it's probably the owner's wish to experience having a litter of kittens in the home at least once and this is transferred to his cat.

The Female in Heat

The female cat becomes sexually mature between the sixth and the twelfth month of life and then is in heat two to three times a year. She will leave anyone who hasn't yet realized that she's gotten into the mood for marriage, no doubt about it. She expresses it unmistakeably. The mating season, which is also referred to as estrus, rut, or heat and which lasts for 15 to 21 days, can be expected to occur twice a year, around the beginning of March and the beginning of June. During this period, the still inexperienced cat owner should be prepared for anything.

The cat wanders restlessly through the apartment, rubs up against her people's legs, purrs, constantly makes little noises, and insists on being stroked. But this still doesn't satisfy her for long. Increasingly restless, she rolls back and forth on the floor, meows and screams the soul out of her body for the tomcat. If her longing is not satisfied, she sings her love song, which is not unlike the crying of a small child, almost uninterruptedly. The exotics, particularly, such as the Siamese (see Portraits of Favorite Purebred Cats, pages 116 to 137), have unbelievably powerful voices and absolutely shameless lack of restraint when it comes to displaying their drive. My Burmese cat Nina gets completely out of control. She no longer eats, rolls ceaselessly from one side to the other with sinuous movements, and "presents" herself to everyone with raised rear end and tail bent to one side. All the while she produces sounds whose resounding depths one can only marvel at.

The Tomcat on the Trail of Love

The tomcat is no less driven. He is irresistably drawn out on the search for female cats. In the house he rages about, scratching at windows and doors to be let out, and everywhere he leaves behind his scent marking. In short, it's unbearable. Neutering (see page 36) is the only remedy for it. Outside, the tomcat covers a wide territory, diligently spraying his urine with its scent, doesn't come home at night, meows and yowls, grumbles and growls and fights with other tomcats for the favors of a lady. When I arrived at my Italian vacation home in the middle of April, all the female cats were prowling around with fat bellies and exhibited no more interest in the male sex. Meanwhile the tomcats stalked through the area as hungry for love as before. Because they are ready to mate at almost any time of year, they look for female cats everywhere. My neighbor tomcat was very much interested in both my females and simply plastered the stair landing at our front door with his scent. But, alas, all his meowing and yowling was love in vain, for Matilda has been spayed.

The mood for love. Enraptured the tomcat rolls on his back. Obviously he has perceived the scent of a female in heat, which has aroused him sexually.

Foreplay—A Rigorous Ritual

The choice of tomcat is entirely a female matter. Therefore if you introduce a tomcat to your female at home, it can happen that she'll reject him. There's nothing to be done then and you must look around for a new candidate.

In spite of the desire on both sides, the affair is carried out according to a rigorous ritual, for it is difficult for the solitary female to allow a stranger to approach without further ado. Though the cat has acted so "man-crazy" before, now she takes her time, if only to see if admirers more to her taste might show up. Quietly she sits there some distance away and is also not particularly impressed if the tomcats' spitting and circling come to blows with each other. She by no means chooses to give herself to the victor of such encounters. The loser also may have a chance with her, and the other cats respect that.

When the one she has selected with enticing meows approaches her, she retreats from him at first, and if he's aggressive, she may even defend herself with swipes of her paws. This behavior is known as "coquettish flight," for she doesn't go far. As soon as she's gotten some distance away, she rolls provocatively and lures him to her again with encouraging sounds. This pattern is repeated several times and serves step by step to overcome the deeply rooted defense need before mating takes place.

When male and female have been kept together for a long time, this complicated foreplay is no longer required. It's possible you may hardly even be aware of it because both cats are comfortable with each other beforehand and the mating is completed with less noise and more gently.

Mating

When the female finally consents to the male's wooing, she crouches, lays her tail to one side, and makes treading movements with her hind legs. The tomcat mounts her, grabs her by the nape of the neck, and growling, completes the mating with a couple of thrusts. Immediately thereafter the semen is ejected, which the female accompanies with a piercing shriek. Thereupon the tomcat leaps away in a bound, for usually the female will give him a box on the ears.

This grabbing by the neck appears very brutal, of course, but it may serve the purpose of keeping the female completely still at the moment of copulation, something like the carrying posture into which little kittens fall when the mother cat carries them around by the neck.

Also the cry the female cat utters as soon as the male pulls his penis from her vagina and the angry swats she tries to give him have their plausible grounds. It has been discovered that the penis is armed with barbs, which lie flat when entering but are erected on withdrawal and scratch the walls of the vagina painfully. This "shock" is necessary, for through it the ovum is set in motion and fertilization becomes possible.

After copulation, the male and female move some distance from each other and lick their genitals. Within a short time, however, the female is again in the mood—she's already forgotten the pain—and is twisting and rolling anew, so that it doesn't stop with one mating. Moreover the cat can mate with still other tomcats and it is thus possible that she can bear kittens from different fathers.

Breeding Purebred Cats

When I wanted to have my purebred Burmese Nina mated, I wasn't even thinking about breeding, but because she is not only pretty but also a particularly loving and charming cat, I didn't have an easy time of choosing a tomcat. Moreover, the choice of place isn't so easy sometimes, and you may have to make a long journey, for contrary to custom, in breeding, the tomcat is the pasha to whom the female must be brought.

What You Should Think About Beforehand
• Don't have your cat mated just at the first period of heat. She must be at least one year old, long-haired cats even somewhat older.

Opposite page: Chartreuse male, British Shorthair, blue, a successful stud cat. Anyone who wants to breed purebred cats must be aware that he must take his female to the stud cat. With rare breeds, this sometimes can involve quite a journey.

- Obviously the certificate for all immunizations must be completed (see page 61), even for leukemia.
- If you want to have the cat mated for breeding purposes, you must be a member of a breed society and have the documentation of pedigree that is required for all breeding animals. This is the only way you can get papers for your kittens.
- According to breeding rules, your breeding cat may only have litters two times a year at most and can only be mated again three months after her last litter.
- There are also stringent requirements in effect for the kittens. They must be reported to the society within four weeks and may only be given up for adoption after the age of three months. Until then you must bestow much care and time on them and have them wormed and inoculated by a veterinarian.
- It can happen that your female isn't madly in love with the tomcat or that even after a successful mating she doesn't become pregnant. The journey to the tomcat is already filled with stress, and in addition there are the strange surroundings, to which many cats may react sensitively in their own way.

The Choice of Stud Cat

If you don't intend to breed, the choice isn't so difficult. The best thing to do is call the local purebred breed society. There someone probably will know of an owner of an unregistered animal that is handsome and presumably also can give evidence of handsome offspring.

If you intend to breed, you must bear in mind the following:
- The stud cat must be registered; a certificate of registered tomcats of all breeds is available from the pedigreed cat breed society.
- With an accepted stud cat, the cover charges run between $50 and $150 (sometimes even higher); in addition there will be the costs of travel and hotel if he lives in a different city. For, as we have said, you must take the female to the male.
- At the first signs of estrus, notify the owner of the male cat so that the date is not booked for another cat. On the third day of estrus, take your female to the stud cat so that the animals have time to get used to each other. Mating is likely to succeed from the fourth day on.
- In the choice of a stud cat you should be sure to balance good and bad points with reference to the breed standard. For example, the Burmese cat should have intense yellow eyes. If yours cannot demonstrate this characteristic, this bad point can be balanced by having the right eye color in the male.

But only when you have offspring will you be able to tell whether what you calculated from the pedigree and inspection will in fact happen, that is, whether male and female do well together. If the answer is yes, it's advisable to stick with this "marriage."

C hanging to a new nest, which the mother cat undertakes with her babies somewhere between the 20th and 30th day of life, is another relic of her wild past. Probably this behavior is connected with the fact that the kittens gradually must get used to solid food. Therefore the mother cat looks for a nest that offers the greatest possible proximity to the food supply. This need to move is still in the blood of the domesticated cat, even if she need no longer worry about the provision of food.

Pregnancy

How to recognize it: It takes about three to four weeks before you can reliably be sure if your cat is pregnant. Then her nipples begin to turn pink and become erect, and the belly fur surrounding them becomes increasingly sparse. The kittens are about 1 inch (2.5 cm) long and grow quickly from now on. With careful palpation you can even feel them. However, I advise beginners to keep hands off, because with unskilled palpation they can do damage to the kittens. If, for instance, you want to be certain your purebred cat is pregnant, you'd better let the veterinarian confirm it.

How the cat behaves: During this period she's especially devoted to her people. If she's allowed outdoors, she doesn't get too far from the house anymore and returns quickly to her favorite little spot. But because she does need fresh air and exercise too just now, you should urge her to get it and regularly make a few rounds with her. From the fifth week, when her sides begin to fill out and her belly grows ever rounder, the cat will become somewhat more languid anyhow, but you should keep her from making jumps from very high places. Otherwise, everything goes along as usual.

What and how much she eats: A pregnant cat must receive not more food but more nutritious food. Because she is hungry more often, give it to her divided up in smaller portions throughout the day. Primarily she needs protein-rich food in the form of lean fresh meat, cottage cheese, egg yolk, wheat flakes, and grated mild hard cheese. In addition, she needs a calcium and vitamin preparation that you had best let the veterinarian recommend.

Where she gives birth: From about the fifth week, the cat begins looking for a nest. She searches through the house, burrowing around in chests, drawers, and baskets and inspecting the most remarkable places as long as they seem to her to be remote and quiet. She also will extend her search outdoors, and therefore you should begin to offer her an appropriate birthing spot.

What you can do: It's best to choose a basket, a firm cardboard carton, or a box 12 x 20 inches (30 x 50 cm) in size, with an 8- to 10-inch (20 to 25 cm) high edge. The cat should have room enough to be comfortable but still be able to brace with her back and feet during the birth.

There's no promising your cat will accept this birthing nest. If you keep leading her to it over and over, she perhaps may venture in. If instead she chooses the dark corner of a closet, for example, you can put the box there. Place a firm cushion in it that has been covered with a washable cover, lay a thick layer of newspapers over that, and cover it all with a clean cloth. Usually the cat will then scratch the cloth up to make a comfortable hollow. My Meow-Meow finally decided to have her kittens in the laundry basket. In a case like this, only move the cat when all the kittens have been born.

Burmese kitten. The coat of a kitten frequently does not have the coloration and markings demanded by the Standard. Also the eye color is not yet that of the adult cat.

Havana tomcat. For breeding of purebred cats the only animals permitted are those who possess correct breeding lines for the appropriate family tree.

Introduction, Advice, and Tips

On these pages you'll find all the information that can be important and helpful on the subject of the birth of kittens.

Birth Date

You can figure the birth date yourself: one mating day plus 63 days. Variations of up to seven days before or after occur, but are not alarming. It can happen, however, that you aren't in on the event at all because your cat hasn't let you observe. In general she will give birth easily and is her own midwife. Don't let your outdoor cat outside for 14 days before the birth date without keeping an eye on her. For in spite of her devotion to people, somehow she always is torn between her compulsion to have her kittens unobserved in a secret place and the wish to have approval from you.

Note: Find out from the veterinarian or breeder what you can do if complications arise during the birth. If the birth occurs at night—which is usually the case—you should know ahead of time which veterinarian can be called for help. If there is an animal hospital in the area, there will be an emergency room there.

Before the birth

Picture 1
The cat will let you know by her restless behavior when it is time. She meows lightly and complainingly, runs along behind you, then back to her birthing box again or scratches around in the litter box without using it.

What you can do: Lead her to her birthing nest and talk gently to her, and she finally will lie down. A devoted cat will demand your presence. But don't press her and behave calmly and levelheadedly. Nervousness and excitement will only be transmitted to the cat and will upset her.

During the Birth

Pictures 2 and 3
It can last for hours, sometimes even be drawn out over a whole day. The first kitten can be expected some two to three hours after the first labor pain.

What you can do: Only interfere if it's really necessary. Especially if your cat is having kittens for the first time, she is very nervous. Stay with her, reassure her with gentle talking and tender stroking. You also can hold your hand against her back

1) Two days before the birth the cat has gotten used to the birthing nest prepared for her. The basket or box should be large enough so that she can stretch out comfortably in it.

so that she can brace against it when pushing.

Crouching or lying on her side, the cat expels the kitten. As soon as it comes into the light of the world, the mother licks it clean and thus stimulates breathing to begin. When the placenta is expelled, the cat bites the umbilical cord close to the body of the kitten and eats it, along with the afterbirth. There are important nutrients and minerals contained in it that help her recover from the strain of the birth. After some 30 minutes, the next contraction starts for the second kitten. Things go along in this rhythm until all the young are born.

After the Birth
Picture 4
The kittens scarcely have recovered from the effort of coming into the world when they begin to struggle toward the source of milk. They are still blind and deaf, of course, but they can already smell. Whether it's the sense of smell that directs them or simply the warmth and blind feeling about, anyhow they always find what they're looking for.

What you can do: When the cat finally is lying on her side and purring comfortably and the kittens are hanging on her nipples like burrs, you can carefully draw the cloth and the newspapers out from under her. Then the cat family can lie there on the covered cushion, clean and dry.

Keeping Warm
Newborn kittens need warmth above all. Sometimes it can happen that the mother doesn't give them enough. You can read it when a cat mother doesn't know what she has to do, for then she gives an impression of confusion and

2) As soon as the amniotic sac containing the baby is expelled, the mother tears the sac open.

3) Initiation of breathing is stimulated by vigorous licking.

depression. On the other hand, if all goes as it should, she will appear quiet and contented. The best way to warm newborn kittens is to put them on a wool blanket with a hot water bottle (100.4° F [38° C]) underneath. In addition you can install an infrared lamp over the nest (31 inches [80 cm] away). Now and again it happens that a kitten falls out of the nest and the mother doesn't retrieve it. In order to warm it up quickly, stick it in a wool sock and put it back at the nipple again. Drinking and cuddling with its siblings is very important now.

4) Purring comfortably, the cat lies on her side while the kittens grope blindly for the source of milk.

The First Days and Weeks
Newborn kittens are blind and deaf but they already have a complete coat. The development up to 12 weeks is described on these pages.

Week 1
Pictures 1 and 2
Toby is three days old, about 6 inches (15 cm) long and weighs between 4 ounces and a little over 5 ounces (120 and 150 g). His eyes are still closed, his tiny little ears are folded shut. He sleeps a lot and drinks often at his favorite nipple, which he recognizes by the scent. There he already has begun "milk kneading." Maddy is Toby's sister. She was born an hour later than he was. To stimulate digestion, the mother licks the belly and then finally the anus clean.

Week 2
Picture 4
By this time Maddy has doubled her birth weight. But her little legs are still too weak to lift her fat tummy off the ground, and she keeps rolling around. Her eyes are open now, and her ears are erect. If her mother isn't there, she and her brothers sleep in a dense tangle. They already can purr like experts but they also can meow piteously, especially when they feel abandoned by their mother.

Week 3
Picture 5
The kittens are growing and now weigh four times their

80

birth weight. But still their legs are not long enough to hold up their fat tummies. Once the kittens have their muscles under control, they can stand on their feet and take the first wobbly steps. At the end of the third week they can be given their first solid food and the litter box can be placed next to the nursery box.

Week 4
Toby and Maddy are about to "move." Abruptly their mother takes them by the neck, one after the other, and carries them to another nest. Now the kittens play with each other and clumsily stumble after their tails from every side. They jump and try to climb out of the box. Strang-

1) At three days, the kitten is still blind and deaf.

2) The mother keeps licking the kitten clean.

ers are greeted with hissing and ears laid back.

Weeks 6 to 8
Picture 3
Toby and his sisters can now box, arch their backs, leap, clean themselves, and use the litter box. The position reflex develops, that is the ability to land on all fours after a fall. Toby's zeal for hunting is so great that he once growlingly defended a toy he'd captured.

Month 3
The mother wards off all attempts to nurse with a swat of her paw. Now the kittens must make do with what's in their dish or catch some prey for themselves. Soon they will be given to their new owners, but first they must get their shots.

Raising a Kitten Without a Mother
Sometimes the mother dies after birth or she can't provide enough for the kittens for one reason or another. Because a cat will willingly raise strange young just as if they were her own, it's best to look for a feline wet nurse. If you want to try to bottle-feed the kittens yourself, follow these tips:

Maintenance: Place a basket or carton in a warm, draft-free place and spread it with absorbent wood shavings. For the first two weeks of life, provide constant warmth of between 77 and 86° F (25 and 30° C), perhaps with a heating pad or an infrared lamp; afterward, up to six weeks, reduce the environmental warmth to 68° F (20° C). From three weeks on, place the litter box nearby.

3) *Small cats are always hungry. From about the fifth to sixth week they begin to eat on their own.*

Feeding: Feed milk in a baby bottle or with an eye-dropper (medicine bottle) or with a hypodermic (without needle!). Sterilize before using as for babies. Warm the milk to about 100.4° F (38° C) (lip test), hold the kitten on your lap, grasping it carefully around the neck, and slowly push the nipple into its little mouth. Before and if necessary after each feeding, lightly stroke the kitten's anus and sex openings with toilet paper; massage the belly a little more firmly. Wipe away urine and stool and rub the anal opening with vaseline. The kittens must be burped like babies after they've drunk. Very important! Keep track of daily weight gain.

Diet
- Prepared formula, for instance Borden's KMR from the pet store. You always should have some formula milk and a doll-sized baby bottle with a nipple or Pet-Nip (available at pet stores) on hand whenever kittens are due.
- Partially adapted nursing formula (use double the quantities indicated for infants).
- Hypoallergenic nursing formula.

Note: Kittens cannot tolerate cow's milk because its milk sugar content is too high. Sheep's milk is very good.

Weaning: The switch to solid food begins around week three. At first, mix a half teaspoon of appropriate baby food, some meat juice or veal broth, into the bottle feeding, and then bit by bit keep increasing the portion of solid food (cottage cheese, hamburger, rice gruel with beef or veal baby food) up until week eight, by which time the normally raised kittens will have been weaned by the mother.

4) *The kitten still sleeps many hours a day.*

5) *The kitten meows when the mother leaves the nest.*

81

Learning to Understand Cats

Much about the cat is amazing, for instance the fact that they can lead a "double life," so to speak. At home the cat remains one's cat child, or so it is looked upon by the owner. Yet it's scarcely outside but it acts completely grown-up, is its own master, a free, wild animal, alert and seeking no help from strangers. It is dependent on the human, but when it has succeeded in getting that human to open the door, it's off and away with never a backward look.

One of the great misconceptions that prevails about cats is indicated in the saying "treacherous cat." On this score behavioral researcher Konrad Lorenz writes: "There are few animals in whose face the observant person can so clearly read the mood of the moment as in that of the cat." You must of course be observant to realize why a cat who just before has sat there apparently peaceably gives its friendly neighbor a swat on the nose with a clawed paw. She has signaled it in every way. With eyes, ears, tail, yes, even with her whiskers.

Learning to understand cats means, therefore, thorough knowledge of the variously functioning body parts and sense organs to decode their signals and to get along better with them.

The Cat's Body—An Instrument Perfected for the Hunt

Nothing has changed on the long road of domestication from 3500 years ago until now. Then cats chased rats and mice and there were more than enough of them in the grain stores of humans. Today they don't do anything different. They hunt rats and mice the same as ever, even when they are the most pampered of house pets, whenever they have the opportunity. However good friends they may have gotten to be with such an animal, if they hear it rustling and squeaking anywhere, their hunting drive is awakened.

In addition there's the fact that the modern cat is scarcely different from the wild cat of those times. Since the wild fallow cat turned into a house cat in the New Kingdom of Egypt, it has changed only minimally. It preserved much of its wild heritage and still has it in common with its wild relatives. Now, as ever, the family of cats *(Felidae)* constitutes a very uniform group, and each cat, whether large or small, is immediately recognizable as such and can be confused with no other animal.

Double spread on previous pages: Nosing the whipped cream. Father and son are ready for some mischief.

Body Build—A Fascinating Development

I have no intention of boring you in this section with an enumeration of various bones. The end product is fascinating, namely a muscular body that enables the cat to move in remarkably diverse ways. For sleeping, it rolls up in a tight ball with its head characteristically placed on its side. When it wakes it stretches and lolls with fervor and ends this stretching exercise, which is supposed to stimulate the circulation, by arching its back. The slow, measured tread with which it makes its way to the feeding bowl betrays nothing of the tension-laden stalking step into which it falls as soon as the slightest likelihood of prey is signaled. Not to mention the litheness with which it slips through cracks and holes, flattening itself like a pancake to squeeze under chests of drawers or under a fence.

The cat owes this incomparable fluidity to a flexible skeleton, light, strong bones, and more than 500 muscles (the much larger human has only 650). With them the cat can even move both halves of its body in opposing directions, for instance when it wants to squeeze into a drawer that is only open a crack from above. And who hasn't marveled at the dreamlike certainty with which the cat delicately places paw after paw, balancing on the narrow rail of a fence.

Limbs—What the Cat Can Do with Them

Running: Normally the cat trots along comfortably. When stalking, it moves extremely slowly and under control; it can halt in the middle of a step and freeze in this position for a long time. If its mind is fixed on a goal, its step is more businesslike. When the cat springs for a prize or if it must run from a dog, it can start off like a pistol shot but it can't maintain the speed for long.

Leaping: The cat can jump five times as high as it is large. Usually it does it from a standing position and evaluates the distance precisely so that it lands where it intended to. It com-

Leaping up. While the cat is pressing down with its back legs, the front legs still are drawn in. In the leap they are stretched forward full length, until the front feet have reached the intended goal. Meanwhile the tail is used for steering.

pletes the pounce after prey with outstretched front paws and unsheathed claws. When the cat is surprised, it sometimes leaps backward on all four feet. When leaping down, it usually bends down as far as possible in order to shorten the distance and decreases the impact through bouncing.

Climbing: A cat climbs a tree by springing up the first segment, holding on with its needle-sharp claws and using them like climbing irons, moving quickly upward with the front and rear legs. Now and again it happens that in the urgency of the moment it dares to go too high. Suddenly the cat becomes aware of the height and remains stuck there as if rooted, meowing piteously. Sometimes the fire department is called in as a last resort.

The cat tries first to descend head first. This merely becomes a helpless slide because the back-curving claws don't offer a hold. It works better when the cat climbs down backwards, but that really has to be learned; young cats have difficulty with it at first.

Paws—Walking on Soft Soles

Only the cat's toes touch the floor when it walks. And this quiet walking-on-tiptoes effect is reinforced by the pillowy ball of its foot. This doesn't keep the cat from standing firmly with all four toe tips on the ground. Let the cat balance on your thigh sometime. It's as if four pencils were boring into your skin. These paws so soft to the touch have needle-sharp claws, which on the front feet are retractable. And don't think the cat always walks on soft feet. It also can stamp as if it were wearing hobnailed boots.

Tail—The Barometer of Mood

The tail is the cat's organ of balance and barometer of mood (see page 90). As necessary, the cat uses it with virtuosity for balancing, like a tightrope walker and his pole, for long leaps or free-falls like an airman and his rudder, for the expression of mood like the human and his speech.

Coat—The "Suit" Made to Measure

The coat is both ornament and protection. Its coloration and marking are different in every cat. Its warmth and softness produce pleasant feelings in young and old. The cat is unique in this. For it, the coat and the loosely fitting skin are the "clothes" cut exactly to measure. The coat protects the cat from minor wounds and regulates the body temperature. In summer it is thin, in winter thick, a condition that is of course less noticeable in the indoor cat. And the coat shows something else, too: powerful excitement. At such times, the body and tail hairs are erected, which can mean either aggression or fear.

Licking the coat means much more than cleaning. By means of tireless licking, the cat keeps its fur soft so that it doesn't lose its insulating effect. When the weather is hot, the cat diligently distributes as much saliva as possible over the coat. Because it has no sweat glands, this allows cooling through evaporation.

One of the reasons the modern cat is scarcely different from its ancestor, the wild fallow cat, may be that it doesn't appear to be useful for anything but mousing. Dogs are bred for hunting, herding, pulling, or watching and for these reasons have undergone engineered changes. With cats, on the other hand, the issue was only beauty, not function. Because of their independent character, nothing else would probably work with them.

Leaping down. At first it looks as though the cat were going to run down the wall. In fact it lets itself down a body length, then stretches its body and front legs foward as far as they will go and propels itself vigorously away from the wall in order to have room for its hind legs in landing. On landing, the body contracts itself to take the impact. Here too the tail takes over the steering.

Grooming the coat also serves the cat as a relief from tension, excitement, or embarrassment. This is called "displacement grooming."

How the Cat's Sense Organs Function

The most fascinating thing about cats is their eyes, large lakes of amber-yellow, copper, violet blue, or emerald green. The ancient Egyptians gave special honor to the cat's eyes glowing in the dark, because they believed that they reflected sunlight and protected humankind from darkness.

Seeing—Why the Cat Has Such Big Eyes

For cats, staring each other in the eye is a sign of aggression. Before tomcats rush at each other in a fight, they confront each other motionless for minutes at a time without taking their eyes off each other. For this reason a cat blinks or turns away when you look directly into its eyes, since the cat isn't at that moment in the mood for hostile confrontation.

The size of their eyes provides cats with a kind of overall view, that is they can see everything that moves behind their ears by just looking to the left or right. To distinguish whether it's a leaf moved by the wind or a mouse, however, the cat must turn its head and sharpen the focus of its eyes. As a hunter, it is only interested in anything that moves; it overlooks the unmoving. So in the area where its depth perception is best (between 6 ½ and 20 feet [2 and 6 m]), it can even perceive the bustling ant, whereas a mouse stopped dead still might possibly escape its sight.

That the cat can see almost as well at night as it can in the daytime is almost a cliché. Cats' eyes are adapted to see when there is little light (a sixth of what the human needs) and accomplish this by a mechanism that humans had to invent painstakingly for photographic equipment. So in the darkness the pupils can become enormous and gather a maximum of light. The brighter it is, the more they narrow until the light can only enter the eye through two tiny openings above and below.

Cats' eyes that encounter light in darkness shine like lamps. This effect is produced by a reflective layer at the back of the eye (see Tapetum lucidum, Glossary, page 110). It reinforces the effect of light falling on it so that the cat still can see when we no longer can see a hand before our face.

Hearing—How the Cat Recognizes Mice

"One must have the ears of a cat to be able to distinguish between the voices of the ant and the June bug," wrote a poet. In fact cats have hearing capacity over a range that we can't even dream of. Or can you imagine being able to distinguish the squeaking of tiny mouse voices, the scampering of tiny mouse feet, or the gnawing of delicate mouse teeth from the concert of all the sounds that surround us?

Technically speaking, cats' ears are large, movable sound trumpets that can be directed toward any sound independently of one another. They are capable of hearing frequency ranges up to 65 kHz, humans only up to 20 kHz.

Feeling— How the Cat "Sees" Even in the Dark

It's said that if we were to cut off a cat's whiskers it no longer could slip through a hole. For cats measure the width of an opening with these sensitive feelers and thus know that they will not get stuck. The whiskers are the guide system that leads them around every obstacle in the darkness and signals the body outlines of their catch to them so they can place the death bite properly. *Vibrissae,* as they are called technically, also are located over the eyes, on the chin, and on the backs of the front legs.

Smelling—How the Cat "Takes a Picture" with its Nose

Perhaps you've observed the following scene sometime: Your cat strolls casually through the yard. Suddenly it stops and makes a face that is "silly" and at the same time one of distaste. Then it stretches its head forward, opens its mouth, and pulls back its upper lip. Perhaps the scent of catnip has just reached its nose or, if your cat is a tomcat, the enticing scent of a lady cat in heat. The technical word for this behavior is *flehmen,* a kind of smell-tasting, which cats are enabled to do through a special organ, the Jacobson's organ. It sends the scent information to the brain, which brings about the cat's reaction. In the case of catnip, this is an ecstatic condition, a regular rapture (see Glossary, page 103).

Where we rely on our eyes, the cat employs its nose. With its sense of smell it takes a picture, so to speak, of every new person, every strange cat, every piece of furniture or other object, and of course of its food. A newborn kitten, which is still blind and deaf, can sniff out the nest or the nipple it chose the last time.

The first contact between two cats occurs nose to nose. After that they turn to the anal region. By rubbing with head, chin, and tail, where there are scent glands, cats leave behind the circumstances of their personal "news," which can be "read" by other cats. Although these scent markings are not perceptible to human noses, the urine sprays of unneutered males are, all the more unpleasantly. But it also can happen that your puss who has stretched her nose to your face in such a friendly way will withdraw with distaste because you have tried out a new aftershave lotion.

Tasting—Why the Cat Nibbles

This sense is said not to be so well developed in a cat, at least not with the breadth of variation that we humans enjoy. Probably a cat becomes addicted to particular food less because of taste than from custom and because the smell pleases it more. However, it has been proven through experiments that cats can distinguish salty from unsalty. They have no particular taste for sweet. Therefore the reason for licking the whipped-cream cake on the table is not because the cat has a sweet tooth.

The tongue is the organ of taste. When the cat drinks milk or water, the tongue can be shaped like a little spoon and thus the liquid is scooped into the mouth. Besides, the tongue is the "wash cloth" with which the cat cleans its coat of dust and dirt. This cleaning effect is reinforced by the *Papillae filiformes,* little horny projections in the middle of the tongue that are curved toward the back. This is why the cat's tongue feels like sandpaper.

The Matter of Balance
"He always falls on his feet like a cat," goes the saying. A marvelous characteristic, which gives the cat an advantage over many other animals. The organ of balance in the inner ear is responsible for reporting all important information to the brain. This then provides for taking the right position, but also for a lightning-quick correction, if the cat falls backward, for example. Then the order goes out: Assume normal position, that is the cat turns in free-fall, using the tail as rudder and brake, at first the front of the body, then the rear, curves the back in order to weaken the impact, and lands on all fours.

Cat Talk—A Combination of Body Language and Sounds

Now and then we, as human partners, are quite at a loss because once again we haven't understood why the cat that was just now a submissive, flexible bundle of fur suddenly has turned into a raging predator. For the cat's action is its speech. It expresses with its body what we need words for. In addition it utters noises that express its particular mood in sound.

While I was writing this section the following happened: Matilda sprang softly meowing onto my lap, snuggled possessively against me, and began purring. It almost sounded as if she wanted to say, "My dear, if you don't understand that, you're pretty dumb."

With the following descriptions I'd like to try to sharpen your eye for cat talk so that in the future you can understand what your cat is trying to say to you.

Contentment
The cat sits there with a friendly, relaxed expression. The ears are forward and aimed slightly outward, the whiskers are bristling sideways and fanned out a little. The eyes look calm and blink at the brightness. Or the cat comes meowing up to you and greets you with tail held high and head raised. If you then sit in your chair, it immediately springs into your lap, shoves and pushes until your legs and tummy have assumed the position that is comfortable for it, and begins to purr. An embodiment of comfort and contentment whose therapeutic effect scarcely anyone can resist.

Alertness
You don't see from the cat's gaze that a cat is eager. Its large eyes show no expression of feeling at all. But the ears are pricked and aimed directly forward. The whiskers also are pointed

The arching of the cat's back is incorrectly described as a gesture of submission. In the body language of the cat, however, arching signals defense and the command: Leave me alone! If a cat arches its back when facing a dog that it feels is threatening but at the same time rises up on stiffened legs, it is combining two elements of its body language, attack and defense.

Falling. The cat's ability to always land on all fours is proverbial. In phase 1, it turns the front part of the body, with front legs drawn up, against the back part with back legs outspread. In phase 2, it makes exactly the opposite movement, with rear legs drawn up and front ones outspread. In phase 3, it arches its back to weaken the impact, and in phase 4, it lands elastically on the ground. The rudderlike tail clearly can be seen working as an aid to steering. The cat learns this so-called position reflex at about the seventh week of life.

forward and spread wide. Although the cat holds itself very still, its body has the effect of great tension, which generally is only noticeable at the tip of the tail. It twitches back and forth slightly.

Defense

The signs of defense are subtle and a person who doesn't interpret them correctly will endure painful misunderstandings. Puss sits on the radiator with front paws placed delicately next to each other, the tail decorously covering them. Sweet, you think and try to give her a kiss on the nose. But you have overlooked that her ears are laid back, her pupils have grown very large, and the cat with laid-back whiskers is signaling caution. Because you understand nothing, she switches to defensive tactics and either bites you on the nose or claws your face.

Of course the understanding works better between two cats. When Nina doesn't want to go along with Matilda's attempts to approach her, she remains standing with rear legs slightly bent and head lowered, may possibly arch her back and lash her tail back and forth. Her beginning growls turn to hisses, and in case Matilda hasn't been impressed by that, she makes a fearsome spitting sound.

Attack

If possible, you should avoid putting your hand near a crouching cat that exhibits pupils dilated and ears laid sideways. If its fur also is standing out, its tail is whip-ping back and forth, and it is spitting fearsomely, it soon will strike with unsheathed claws and lightning speed.

Matilda's playful invitation to scuffle always begins more or less the same way. On stiffened legs she rises up before Nina, lays her ears back aggressively, spreads her whiskers, and narrows her pupils. Her tail is arched in a hook shape just beyond the base, and its hairs are standing on end so that it looks like a bottle brush. She ducks down at a right angle in front of Nina, without taking her eyes off her, and then throws herself on her. To keep her from being able to grab her by the neck, Nina rolls onto her

back as quick as lightning and parries with teeth and claws. When tomcats fight, they usually stare at each other for minutes at a time first. Yowling and meowing they stand there motionless, only their tail tips twitching back and forth, faster and faster. Such a battle often ends with bloody bite wounds and fringed ears.

Fear

Fear is converted quickly to defense. This should be clear to you if, for example, you want to touch a stray cat. A fearful cat raises its hackles, arches its back, its tail whips back and forth, and its ears are laid back, its pupils become huge, and it may possibly utter a loud screech. It's better to talk soothingly to it and keep your hands away if you don't want to have to treat a couple of bloody scratches.

Cat Vocabulary

This includes words for cat-to-cat understanding as well as those that serve cat-to-human relations.

Cat-to-Cat Understanding
- The long drawn out rising and falling howl, the so-called cat song, is uttered as a threat before battle and is never a "love song"
- The high-level screeching occurs when the opponent has shown himself to be the stronger and the lower ranking one must defend his skin.

Cat-to-Cat-and-Human Understanding
- Purring is the sign of contentment, but also of fear, when the cat has pain and before it dies, to reassure itself, as it were,

- Meowing occurs in all pitches and gradations, for example when a tiny kitten feels abandoned or when a grown-up cat is discontented,
- "Cooing" is a kind of chatter in many variations that cats have available for all possible circumstances of life. The smitten tomcat entices the female in heat with it and vice versa,
- Hissing, spitting, and growling keep opponents at bay. The gabbling that cats utter when they look through the window and see a bird that remains unreachable to them is not addressed to anyone. They begin to complain then and normally chatter their teeth.

Queen in Her Territory

The view of the cat as a loner misleads people into thinking that except for mating, it behaves hostilely to all other cats. I prefer the idea that the cat goes its own way, in the sense that it never allows itself to be dominated. Its pronounced individualism does not keep it from cultivating contacts, however; it merely does so in its discreet, catlike way.

The Primary Home

This expression coined by the behavioral researchers denotes the place where, in its own mind, the cat lives (see Establishing Territory, page 30). If it lives with you in the house, then it will act very secure and at ease in this home. The befriended human will, as it were, be graciously permitted to share the cat's life. Puss will have several comfortable resting places in the house, and if she has a yard at her disposal too, she also will seek out some places there. It doesn't bother her to share her home with other cats, but only if there is room enough for each to be able to get out of the way when the mood arises and to withdraw somewhere snug.

Through some cat-crazy friends, who have at times had as many as five cats, I've been able to observe dominance ranking at work. Paula, the senior one, lays claim to the best sleeping spot. Sometimes one of the other cats will lie down there. Paula appears not to make anything of it, especially as the other usually will retire from the field voluntarily. Otherwise the cats get along well with each other, because each has its own place that is respected by the others.

There is no contest for dominance between my cats. They often lie next to each other, eat from the same dish, and "occupy" their people amicably.

The Larger Territory

The matter of territory is somewhat more difficult. Suppose your cat is a newcomer and has the run of the yard. But perhaps this already has been claimed by one of the cats in the neighborhood. It then soon will come to an altercation, for your cat quickly has let it be known that the area in which its people live also belongs

Playing with the catch. What appears gruesome to humans is a necessity for the cat. It is reducing its inhibition before administering the death bite.

to its "personal property." But of course the cat has to fight for it first. Outside the yard the cat enters foreign territory, but it also only may be no-man's-land, that is the territory in between. Cats have their paths that they use on patrolling expeditions through their territory. These also may be used by other cats, but not at the same time if possible.

Personal meetings are not desired. Possibly you've observed a scene like this when out on a walk. Cat number one has caught your attention because it keeps popping up from the field at the same distance and peering out of the high grass with ears erect. Meanwhile you've arrived at the edge of the woods and sat down under a tree. Suddenly cat number two appears from the woodsy shadows and now trots along the path. All at once she spots cat number one a few yards away. She sits down, the other does too. Politely they wait. Why? So that one of the two can decide to continue on the path. But then they have to pass each other. Rather, they stroll away in opposite directions.

Dealing with Intruders

In principle a cat always has the say in the territory he or she has marked as its own. Tomcats, of course, often hold sway over a territory that is ten times as large as that of a female and therefore they are more tolerant of intruders. Perhaps this only goes for German cats. Italian cats demonstrate far less "hospitality." In any case, since last year my two cats no longer have been able to set foot on the piazza. For in the meantime, the neighboring

"Prey envy." One cat likes to snatch the prey from under the other's nose. Young cats are taught by their mother to catch mice. She drags a mouse past them and the young must learn to take it away from her.

tomcat has become a despotic ruler over his territory and has taught Nina and Matilda fear. They have only to stick their noses over the doorsill when Pucci streaks up like an angry dervish and belabors them with his claws. Because Pucci has the right of possession and is a malevolent tomcat besides, he of course succeeds. If mine did not have such "fine feelings," there certainly would be fierce fighting.

Crying for food.

Begging for food.

Head rubbing.

Invitation to play.

Anxious reserve.

Ready for attack.

Playful paw.

Angry defense.

Bad state.

Friendly mood.

Cat Language

The cat has an abundant vocabulary of expressions. With ears, eyes, and whiskers it signals its mood of the moment. When meowing, snarling, or purring are present in addition, you know just exactly what sort of spirit the cat is in. The cat's means of expression also include its body, its tail, and its fur. For instance, a tail carried high and rolled slightly forward is a sign of contentment and good humor.

Groups of Cats

Here too is a contradiction to the loner cat stereotype. Obviously the cat behaves that way only when it shares a home with you as a pet; semiwild cats, on the other hand, appear to be extremely social. You hear of the gangs of cats that inhabit the Colosseum in Rome or the cemeteries in Paris, and it has been established that in such cat societies the females all perform nursemaid service and nurse and bring up their young in common.

But house cats that go outdoors also have their secrets. For if they have the chance, they betake themselves to secret meeting places at night. "The animals sit close together," writes behavioral researcher Professor Paul Leyhausen, who succeeded in making this discovery, "at distances of 2 to 5 meters [6½ to 16 feet], some even 'fur touching' distance; some lick and rub against each other. They utter very few sounds; rarely one hears suppressed snarling or growling, sees an ear laid back, if one animal gets too close for comfort, but otherwise the faces are quiet and peaceful, yes, even outspokenly friendly." When a few hours have passed, sometimes even the whole night, the group dissolves again.

Cats Among Themselves

Most interesting is probably the "brotherhood of tomcats," an expression that Leyhausen also coined. It refers to the formal order of dominance that exists among tomcats in an area. Up to a certain age young tomcats enjoy a kind of grace period in this brotherhood. They are accepted, in fact even regularly invited to be present, but are not involved in any fighting. It's as if they are being given time to get accustomed to the hardships of tomcat life.

I could observe this really clearly with my cat Morellino. As a Munich indoor cat he was only able to meet other cats in Italy. They sat in a semicircle on the piazza at dusk and lured him with gentle cooing sounds. Rashly he sauntered up to them and greeted each with nose contact. Each, according to his temperament, merely drew his head back or raised a paw without scratching him. One evening he disappeared with them and was not seen for the next three days. When he returned, he appeared glossy and well nourished and not a hair was crooked.

Opposite page: Cat on the bird feeder. Obviously this should be made inaccessible to cats. Don't put the feeder in the vicinity of trees and bushes, and make it unclimbable, for example by fastening empty bottles to the pole.

Glossary

Many interesting ideas have collected around cats— mytho-logically, historically, and in common expressions—and their explanations often are surprising. In this alphabetical listing, you'll also find technical terms that are important in the context of life shared with a cat and that expand your knowledge of this popular house pet.

A

Abyssinian Tabby
Describes the coat color of the Abyssinian cat in which each single hair is banded, with the exception of the hairs on the underbelly. Patterns, stripes, or dark spots (see TABBY) may not appear; these count as faults as indicated in the Standard (see page 114).

Adrenalin
This hormone is secreted by the adrenal glands in anxiety and fear. The pupils open wide and the cat threatens with defensive posture.

African fallow cat
(Felis sylvestris libyca)
Native to North Africa. There when the Egyptians stored their grain in gigantic ware-houses and mice and rats were swarming, the fallow cats were attracted by the excellent hunting grounds and thus to nearness to human beings (see page 9). The fallow cat is slender and dainty, has large ears and a long tail, and is considered an ancestor of our house cats.

Aggressiveness
Can arise from boredom if house cats have too little outlet for their hunting drive (see page 41). Also cats sometimes react to a shock with extreme irritability and even can attack their owners; you then must get help from the veterinarian.

Agouti
Technical term for wild coloration, a very common coat color that appears in wild, house, and purebred cats. The coloring is pro-duced by bicolored or tricol-ored light-dark banding on every single hair, with the tip of the hair always dark. It also is called TICKING.

Ailurophilia/-phobia
The Greek *ailuros* means "cat." Both words are derived from it and mean cat love or cat fear.

Albino
Albino cats have only a little color pigment or none at all and therefore have a snow-white coat, pale pink skin, and light-blue eyes with a red pupil. Albinos often are deaf.

Allergy
It is true that people can have an allergic reaction to cats. Nevertheless, cats may not be to blame for every sud-denly occurring allergy. Only a medical test can determine the cause for sure.

American Shorthair
The ancestress is supposed to have come over on the *Mayflower* in 1620. This breed is similar to the Euro-pean house cat. It is a sturdy, muscular animal with a broad face and splendid set of whiskers.

Angora cats

Popularly all cats with long hair are termed angoras. However, the Turkish Angora (see page 122) is one of the oldest original breeds. These long-haired cat beauties get their name from the Turkish city of Ankara, which at that time was called Angora in Greek.

Animal experiments

Cats have been and are being misused in many areas of scientific research for experiments in which they must suffer great pain. Experimenters consider cats an ideal research subject because they react clearly and measurably to stress and pain.

Avoidance

A term from behavioral science. If a cat doesn't know what to do next in a conflict situation, it suddenly turns to another activity, such as licking itself.

B

Baby coat

Young cats have a thick, soft coat that often does not yet show the marking and coloration demanded by standards for purebred cats, which appears later. This is important when you are buying a purebred kitten. The photographs on pages 116 to 137 show markings of adult cats of the various breeds and the corresponding kitten.

Furthermore, the smooth, shining coat or, depending on breed, the long, silky coat is only fully developed in the adult cat.

Backcrossing

Mating of an animal of the parent generation with an animal of the daughter generation.

Balance

Cats do not get dizzy and can balance on the narrowest railing, though they may be in danger of falling off. If they do not fall from too great or too short a distance, they are saved by their ability to turn in free-fall and land on their feet.

Behavioral disturbances

These can be inherited or acquired. Cats that have had negative experiences in their earliest youth often tend to disturbed behavior as adults when something in their environment changes. Some-times they react to changes that seem insignificant to the cat owner but are unbearable for the cat. Behavioral disturbances range from uncleanliness, timidity, refusal to eat, through fear of being touched and aggres-siveness to severe illness. In this case it's necessary to find out what has knocked the cat off balance. It helps to provide harmony and avoid stressful events, as well as to create a stress-free environ-ment in which the cat can be comfortable again.

Bezoars

Hair balls that develop in the stomach when the cat has swallowed too much hair while licking. Normally the animal vomits it up again. But if the cat does not succeed in doing so, the hair balls block the gut, resulting in obstruc-tion, loss of appetite, listless-ness, and frequent vomiting. In light cases, one-half teaspoon of paraffin or olive oil helps. If there is no improvement, go to the veterinarian.

Black Bombay cat
American breed that is produced by crossing a Burmese and a black American Shorthair. Because of its black coat and its copper-colored eyes, people also call it a "mini panther."

Blinking
A sign of a peaceable mood.

Blue eyes
All kittens have them. In adult cats they are a mark of pedigree, for example in Siamese and Burma breeds (see pages 131 and 126). Blue-eyed cats—especially white ones—often are deaf (see HEREDITARY DISEASES).

Bobtail
See JAPANESE BOBTAIL.

Breeder name
A protected name, recognized by the particular breed association, for cats from a certain breeder; it is entered in a register of breeders' names.

Bristle hairs
Together with the sturdy, long LEAD HAIRS, they make up the COVER HAIRS of the cat's coat.

C

CAC—Certificat d'Aptitude au Championat
Expectation of the title of CHAMPION. See QUALIFICATION.

Cannibalism
Rarely occurs in cats. If a mother cat kills her young and eats them, it happens because of inexperience or because she is very anxious and nervous. A cat that becomes a mother for the first time does not yet know how to bite off the umbilical cord and eats her babies along with it by mistake. It also has been observed that tomcats kill kittens, but the reason is entirely different: Because the nursing mother cat will not allow herself to be mounted, the tomcat turns to the young and, in the attempt to mate, also gives them a neck bite, which unfortunately for the small kitten is also a lethal bite.

Carnivores
The Latin word for all predatory animals, which include our house cat. Alfred Brehm called the cat the most perfect predator of all.

Carrier
Transport cage of plastic that is secure against escape and in which the cat can travel, for instance in an airplane.

Carrying posture
The term for the position into which a kitten automatically falls when its mother picks it up by the neck and carries it around. It drops its tail between its hind legs and curls it

tightly under the body so that it doesn't drag on the ground.

Cat
Refers to a number of other things besides the animal. Some examples are: in the Middle Ages a cat was the name for a movable protective roof under which besiegers stormed a castle. Also fieldworks and covered towerlike structures as well as a storming apparatus with which walls were battered were called cats. Today the implements for demolishing buildings are still called cats.

Catching prey
Kittens learn from their mother. She teaches them how to grab a mouse at the back of the neck with their teeth and shows them the death bite.

Cat litter
A cat likes to cover up after urinating or defecating. Many things can be used as litter: sand, peat, wood shavings, sawdust, even shredded newspaper. Most practical, because it also takes up odors, is ready-to-use litter from the pet store or supermarket. Biodegradable cat litter is especially good because it can be discarded on the compost heap (see pages 26 and 27), thus protecting the environment.

Cat museum
The Riehener Cat Museum (near Basel) was established privately and displays much of the extant lore and knowledge about cats. The collection includes some 10,000

objects and it also will install thematic exhibits from time to time.

Cat music
Term for shrill, monotonous music. It was "invented" in the eighteenth century by students who used it to protest against unpopular professors.

Catnip
Nepeta cataria, also called catmint, is a plant you can raise in your garden if it doesn't already grow wild there. It contains a volatile oil whose scent sends cats into deepest ecstasies. The cats usually go right out of their minds, snuffle the plant, lick and chew on it with increasing fervor, bite into it, rub cheeks and chin, purr loudly, and spring into the air. This condition lasts between five and 15 minutes and is neither good nor harmful for cats. VALERIAN has a similar effect. Experienced cat keepers advise not giving the cat too much catnip or valerian.

Cat wash
Common popular expression for superficial cleaning, which doesn't match reality, because cats wash themselves very thoroughly all over.

Champion
A cat is designated a champion when it has been judged the best of its breed and class in at least three shows.

Chinchilla
This color, appearing only in Persian cats, describes a white coat that gets its ashy-gray sheen from the black

tips of the hairs, or TIPPING. These cats are especially charming because of their emerald- to blue- green "storybook" eyes, which are surrounded by a black "eye line."

Colostrum
Called the first mother's milk, which is particularly rich in protein and antibodies. It is enormously important for newborn kittens to have this milk.

Cooing
A sound in cat language. Your cat uses cooing to communicate with you, announces with a cooing noise that it intends to jump to a high place, lures a timid, shy companion from her hiding place with a cooing sound.

Copulation
Mating between a female cat and tomcat usually lasts for only a few seconds. The female indicates when it is finished (see page 75).

Cover hairs
This is the name for long lead hairs and the shorter, supple bristle hairs of the cat's coat.

D

Deceitful
Always being said of cats, but there can be no talk of deceit. Cats express themselves very clearly if they intend to bite or scratch (see page 92). Anyone who gets scratched or bitten hasn't observed his cat carefully. Only cats with behavioral disturbances are

sometimes unpredictable. Little kittens that scratch someone have yet to learn the difference between cat skin and human skin.

Declawing
Considered by some as animal torture, because the cat without claws can never again hold onto anything and simply slides down helplessly.

Dewclaw
A fifth claw, located on the inside of the front paws, and also is termed "the thumb."

Diabetes
Unfortunately this disease also occurs in cats and expresses itself in loss of appetite or voracious eating, weight loss, great thirst, and vomiting. It also can lead to diabetic coma—that is, fainting attacks or convulsions. In this case, you must give the animal one to two teaspoons of honey or fruit syrup immediately and take it to the veterinarian.

Domestication
The term for the process that continues over many generations of animals through which a house pet evolves from a wild animal.

Dominance ranking
Cats aren't very particular about it, to be sure, but it is observed. At the feeding place the highest-ranking cat may choose the best morsels. It also lays claim to the best sleeping place, which the others also may use at certain times. When two cats meet, the lower-ranking one moves out of the way (see RIGHT OF WAY).

Drooling
Cats "slobber" sometimes when they're being affectionate or are very excited, for instance on a visit to the veterinarian. This is irksome but nothing serious. Constant salivation can be an indication of gum disease, which must be treated by the veterinarian.

E

Elizabethan collar
Placed around a cat's neck after an operation. The

wedge of stiff material is supposed to keep the cat from licking or pulling at the wound or bandage.

Encounter
When two cats meet in strange territory, they first check out the surroundings. Then they greet with nasal and anal contact, with each cat trying to sniff the other first. Whoever succeeds gains "mastery."

European Wildcat
(Felis sylvestris)
Considered one of the original forms of our house cat, it is larger and sturdier than these, and lives in the cooler regions of Europe and Asia Minor. In Germany, they are found in the Harz, Hunsrück, and Eifel regions. Their fur is yellowish-gray with dark, silvery stripes. The tail is long with dark rings and a black tip. Now and again it happens that a female house cat mates with a wildcat. The kittens then have a genetic inheritance from the wildcat.

F

Fallow cat
See AFRICAN FALLOW CAT.

False pregnancy
Through induced OVULATION the cat sometimes will be falsely pregnant, with all the signs, except that an egg has not been fertilized. Usually a cat in such a condition can be a wet nurse for motherless kittens, because she even has a supply of milk.

Felines
(Latin Felidae)
The zoological name for the family of cats. It includes the big cats (Pantherini), the lynxes (Lyncinae), the hunting leopard (Acenonychinae), and the small cats (Felinae).

Felis
The Latin name for house cat.

Fever
The normal body temperature of the cat ranges from 101.3 to 102.2° F (38.5–39° C). A cat has a fever at any point above 102.7° F (39.3° C). It is usually an indication of infection.

FIFE—Fédération Internationale Féline
Umbrella organization for several European cat societies.

Flehmen
The term for a particular expression of the face made, for instance, when the tomcat gets the scent of a female in heat.

Freedom symbol
Way back in ancient Rome, cats were said to lie at the feet of the goddess Libertas. During the French Revolution they also were considered a symbol of freedom because of their independence and free will.

Free-fall
When falling, cats turn from being on their backs to their stomachs, using the tail for steering and braking. This turning happens so quickly that it is scarcely perceptible

to the human eye. Shortly before landing they stretch out all four legs and land safely on all four feet, provided they don't fall from such a height that the landing is too hard or from so short a distance that they haven't time to complete the turning maneuver. The ability to turn in free-fall is called position reflex. It develops at the sixth week of life.

G

GCCF—Governing Council of the Cat Fancy
The umbrella organization of cat breeders of Great Britain.

Ghost marking
In a self-colored cat a marking that shows through—undesirable in a purebred cat.

Grass
It's said that cats need grass to make them vomit the fur swallowed during grooming. At any rate, they like to eat it. If you have available a dish with cat grass (obtainable at the pet store), papyrus, sprouted oat grains, or the old familiar spider plant, they will not go for your houseplants, which are often dangerous for them because they are poisonous.

Greeting
Takes place from cat-to-cat via the nose. When a cat greets "its" people, it rubs against their legs, bumps against them, and keeps giving them numerous HEAD RUBBINGS.

Greeting kiss
The term for the nose-touching with which two friendly cats greet each other. They do it with "their" people too, when they find themselves at nose height.

H

Hair balls
See BEZOARS.

Harlequin cat
A white cat with a few large spots of color in black, red, blue, and tortoiseshell.

Head rubbing
A type of contact. The cat rubs its cheeks or neck against a reachable part of its partner, for example a human leg or the flank of a friendly dog.

Hereditary diseases
These are passed on through the genes; an example is the repeated incidence of deafness in combination with blue eyes in white cats (see HEREDITY).

Heredity
Each cat hands onto its offspring one half of the genes for particular characteristics, for example, for coat or eye color, so that these genes are possessed in duplicate. The laws of heredity were discovered in the middle of the

nineteenth century by the Austrian monk Gregor Mendel. This discovery made possible the development of breeding for particular characteristics.

Homeopathy
Disease preventions, care, and curing with natural agents without stressful side effects is also helpful for cats.

Homing ability
A test at the Zoological Institute at the University of Kiel demonstrated that cats quickly found their way home from distances of 3 miles (5 km) away but not, on the other hand, from 7 miles (12 km). Of course there are cats who find their way home again from hundreds of miles away, but these are the exceptions.

Horizontal ears
Stunting of the ear muscle in the Scottish Fold (see page 134).

Houseplants
These often constitute a danger to cats, because many of them are poisonous. But because cats love to nibble on GRASS, some should be available to them in a shallow dish. As a rule they then will not bother the plants not specifically intended for them. Better still, avoid keeping any poisonous

houseplants, such as: crown of thorns, dumb cane (dieffenbachia), croton, oleander, primula (primrose), poinsettia, desert rose, philodendron.

Hunting drive
Always present in cats, whether they are hungry or satiated. Satisfied cats are said to be even better mousers than hungry ones; thus the hunting drive is not identical with the drive for food.

Hybrids
The technical expression for the offspring of cats of different breeds. Mixed breed or bastard are the layman's terms.

I

Immunizing shots
See SHOTS.

Impressing behavior
This expression from behavioral science is the term for the form of expression with which all cats, but tomcats particularly, try to show their opponent who is superior. It includes arching back, erected fur, laid-back ears, stepping sideways in order to look bigger, or sharpening claws.

Inbreeding
Pursued systematically in order to strengthen particular breed characteristics or genetic traits. But it should only be undertaken by experienced breeders who know their way around genetic science. All too easily one can make mistakes that have severe consequences in future offspring.

J

Jacobson's organ
A sense organ in the gums of the cat (lacking in humans) that can be activated by chemical stimuli and stores up scents.

Japanese Bobtail
Its tiny little stump of tail that looks like a pompom has come about through mutation. They are slender, long-legged, have soft voices, and are said to be especially talkative and intelligent.

K

Kinked tail
It is supposed to be an authentic sign of a Siamese cat. Today people are trying to breed it out. Arises from a developmental defect in the tail vertebrae.

Kneading
Nursing kittens knead the nipples of the mother cat with their front paws to get the milk flow started. Grown cats continue to make these movements, which also are

called treading, when they wish to express a sense of great well-being.

L

Lead hairs
They occur scattered among the COVER HAIRS of the cat, are particularly long and firm, and can be erected by small muscles. The smooth, thin tail of a Burmese cat then looks like a bottle brush.

Lethal factor
(from Latin *letum*, meaning death) Hereditary disease condition that leads to death. The lethal factor in the genetic makeup of the tailless Manx cat, for instance, guarantees one stillbirth in a litter of four kittens.

Life expectancy
Indoor cats can live to be fifteen or even twenty years old. For cats with access to the outdoors, especially because of the danger of traffic, the life expectancy is much less.

Locket
The term for the white neck spot, often the only other color on the fur of the cat.

Loner
Puss gladly shares her house cat existence with her people but also with other cats. She could be called a loner because she is not an animal that travels in a pack.

Lucky cats
In folklore, these are the tricolored and four-colored

tortoiseshells. Thus in Brehm's *Tierleben (Lives of Animals)* it says: "A tricolored cat protects the house from fire and other misfortunes, men from the fever. They also put out the fire if one throws them into it and are therefore called fire cats. Anyone who drowns one will have seven years' bad luck." The business about throwing in the fire should not, of course, be taken literally. In England and Scotland it's black cats that bring luck, in China ones that are particularly old and ugly.

M

Mailing
Cats of course may not be packed in cartons and shipped. Most cats would be so frightened and shocked after the trip through the mails that they would need weeks to recover from the terrifying experience. Always fetch the cat personally and transport it home in a cat basket or CARRIER.

Maltese Cat
The old name for the Chartreuse cat (see page 135).

Manx cat
Comes from the Isle of Man. Probably because of the isolation on the island the characteristic taillessness that arose through mutation could become established. A distinction is made between rumpies and stumpies. The rumpy has a round indentation at the place where a tail

normally would begin; the stumpy has a tiny stump of a tail. Because of the missing tail, the Manx has a rabbit-like, hopping gait. (See LETHAL FACTOR.)

Markings
The term for the dark facial mask and dark ears, paws, and tail in the Siamese, Color point, and Sacred Cat of Burma, for example. Markings are darker than the basic color of the rest of the coat (see POINTS).

Mask
Designates the face marking of some cat breeds, for instance the Siamese. It is very clearly distinguished from the other fur.

May kitten
Spring cats usually are born in May and are considered to be particularly healthy and hardy, probably because they are born in the warmth and light of days that are growing longer.

Miming
Cats are really expressive mimers. When they show their play face, the ears point up, the eyes open wide; in the pleasure face the ears are forward, the eyes half-closed; in a threatening face the ears are laid backward, the pupils narrow, and in a defensive face the ears cock forward, the pupils are opened wide.

Money cat
In the Middle Ages, a common expression for a bag of money.

Mouth odor
Cats have it because of their diet. So avoid feeding too much fish, for example, for the animal will smell of it afterward. Bad breath can indicate infected gums but also other serious disease. The cat must then go to the veterinarian.

Mutation
A genetic change that appears spontaneously and through which the color, hair pattern, or growth form of the cat is altered. The genetic change can be passed on to offspring.

N

Neck bite
Used by cats on different occasions: The mother picks up her kittens (causing CARRYING POSTURE) with a neck bite and carries them to another spot; the tom grabs the female by the neck skin during mating; the death bite is placed in the neck of the prey and must first be learned.

Nesting drive
Occurs several weeks before birth. Then the house cat begins to inspect for suitable birthing places and often seeks out the most remarkable spots if only they appear to offer enough protection for her kittens.

Nictitating membrane
The term for the third eyelid of the cat, which covers the eyeball wholly or partly from the inner corner in situations in which danger threatens, in injury, exhaustion, debility, or dehydration of the organism in disease.

Nose leather
The name for the tip of the nose in cats and other animals. For purebred cats, its color is prescribed by the Standard. In a healthy cat, the nose leather should be cool and damp.

Nurturing drive
The technical term for mother love in the animal kingdom. Cats are known as particularly good mothers, who defend their kittens against even the most aggressive attackers.

O

Odd-eyed
Cats with eyes of a different color, that is one blue eye and one orange eye.

Oily/greasy tail
Can occur with all cats but happens especially with long-haired cats. The glands on the upper side of the tail secrete too much oil, so that the tail looks smeary and yellow-brown. The condition is treated with powder.

Orientation memory
Exists in cats but is still unexplained to a large extent. The fact is that some cats over thousands of miles away from home have found their way to their owners even when they had moved to a completely unfamiliar place.

Origins
The ancestors of our house cats are primarily the AFRICAN FALLOW CAT *(Felis sylvestris libyca)* and the EUROPEAN WILDCAT *(Felis sylvestris).*

Ovulation
From Latin, meaning egg movement. It takes place 24 to 30 hours after copulation. The mature egg now leaves the ovary and is fertilized one to two days later.

P

Panleukopenia
The Latin name for feline distemper.

Papillae
Small bumps on the tongue that sense taste; they make the cat's tongue feel like sandpaper.

Pariah cats
Rejected cats that are on the lowest level of dominance order, are picked on by all, and are driven from the feeding bowl. Such hierarchies usually exist only when cats must live together under too-crowded conditions. If they have freedom to move, they simply avoid each other and so social stratification does not occur.

Picking up
Never pick up a cat by the scruff of the neck. Place one hand under the chest, the other under the rear end to lift it. Only the mother cat knows how to pick her young up by the scruff so that they fall into the CARRYING POSTURE.

Points
Strongly colored MARKINGS on the tips of the body (ears, feet, tail) of the cat that clearly are distinguished from the rest of the coat color.

Poisonous houseplants
See HOUSEPLANTS.

Polydactyly
Having many toes. Cats sometimes can have extra toes and claws, up to ten on each foot. These hereditary malformations don't hinder them at all, but they should not have offspring.

Position reflex
See FREE-FALL.

Purring
How this characteristic, comfortable-sounding cat

sound is made is not completely clear despite research. In Grzimek's *Lives of Animals* it says that small cats have a completely ossified hyoid bone and thus cannot really roar like the big cats. For this reason, they purr with inspiration and expiration.

Purring is considered to be a sign of well-being and a sound of reassurance (mother cats use it to soothe their young). Because suffering and dying cats also often purr, however, it can't only be an expression of well-being. Perhaps the cat is trying to say: "I am peacefully inclined, don't do anything to me."

Putting to sleep
When a cat is old or seriously ill with no hope of improvement, it should be released from pain by a euthanasic injection, which only a veterinarian can administer (see page 44).

Q

Qualification
Validation at shows by recognized breeders. The grades are good, very good, excellent (see CAC).

Quarantine
Isolation measures to protect against rabies. When traveling to England, Malta, Australia, New Zealand, Ireland, Finland, Norway, and Sweden, cats must remain in quarantine for six months. Therefore do not take cats with you when you go to these countries on vacation.

Queen
In England, the term for a breeding cat.

R

Recessive
The name for a latent inherited trait that does not appear in a mixed heritage. It will be expressed only when both parents have the trait.

Relief play
When cats have killed a very large and dangerous prey, a rat for example, they play with it some more after death and fling it around for a while.

Rent law
Many landlords forbid the keeping of cats. This includes the right to house pets as long as no one is injured by them. Unfortunately the legal question is not unambiguous: There are different judgments for or against keeping cats (see page 44).

Rex coat
A wavy or curly coat produced through a recessive MUTATION in which the COVER HAIRS are wholly or partly missing.

Right of way
One cat will give another right of way in its territory, provided they know each other. Strangers to the area will be chased off. In such encounters a direct confrontation is avoided. Both cats wait "politely" at a certain distance, and then the higher-ranking one is allowed to go first. Nevertheless if the lower-ranking one was there

first, it may continue on its way. Again, the high social development of cats is seen in such behavior.

Rumpy
Completely tailless MANX CAT.

S

Scent marking
Cats leave their scent on trees, bushes, walls, or furniture to mark their territories. To do so they stand with their rear ends in front of the object and spray it with a fine spray of urine. Cats in heat also leave scent markings to entice their suitors. What cats smell with pleasure usually is almost unbearable for humans. Neutered cats mark with urine far less. The markings cats make with feet and chin (see page 34) are not perceptible to the human nose.

Sex determination
In a tomcat, the distance between anus and sexual organs is larger than that in the female cat. The sexual opening itself is round in the male, elongated in the female.

Shots
An absolutely necessary precautionary health measure, because they immunize cats against the most lethal viral diseases, feline distem-

per, feline pneumonitis, rabies, and feline leukemia (see page 61).

Speed
For short distances, the house cat can get up to a speed of 30 mph (48 kmh). Leopards can do up to 69 mph (112 kmh) and are thus the fastest animals in the world.

Spitting
Cats spit when they feel threatened and this announces that they will defend themselves.

Spotting
White spots, which range from a small white neck spot (see LOCKET) to all over.

Sterility
Now and again this also occurs in cats. The causes can be various. In males sometimes it's genetically determined. In females it may be caused by improper diet with too few vitamins and minerals, by an inflammation of the uterus, or an infection in the genitals.

Stop
The interval between the forehead and the tip of the nose. It is especially pronounced in the Persian, that is to say, seen in profile, the Persian has a very sharp bend there.

Stress
Produced in unusual situations, for instance when the cat undergoes change of owner, separation of the young cat from its mother, at shows, or on trips, causing the metabolism to be accelerated and through that the danger of infection increases.

Superstition
All sorts of superstitions have become entwined around cats. Thus we usually consider a black cat a bringer of bad luck; on the other hand a tricolored or four-colored one is considered a protectress of the home and a bringer of good luck. Cats also are seen as weather prophets and mascots, being supposed to ensure a lucky voyage on a ship, for example.

Sweating
Cats don't sweat all over their body like humans, but they do have sweat glands between the toes and the balls of the feet, on the lips, at the corners of the chin, in the region of the nipples and the anus. In great excitement or tremendous heat, they open their mouths and pant.

T

Tabby
A term for a coat pattern. Four groups are distinguished: Mackerel tabby—tiger-striped pattern; blotched tabby—flecked pattern; spotted tabby; ABYSSINIAN TABBY—no pattern.

Tail
It's a balancing pole, steering mechanism (see FREE-FALL), and mood barometer (see page 86) all in one.

Tapetum lucidum
Phosphorescent layer at the back of the eye of the cat. In darkness it makes the eye reflective.

Teeth
Young cats up to six months old have a set of milk teeth with 26 teeth. The adult cat has 30 teeth.

Teeth change
Usually occurs uneventfully and without complication at the age of 24 weeks.

Threat posture
Before a cat scratches or bites, it announces its intention through threat posture. Pupils close to a narrow slit, ears stiffen and are slightly laid back, the tail lashes back and forth. A cat stares threateningly at a cat opponent with its body positioned sideways—a friendly cat does not look another in the eyes—and at the same time the cat utters a rising and falling cat song.

Ticking
Technical term for the dark banding of every individual hair, for example, in the Abyssinian cat (see ABYSSINIAN TABBY).

Tipping
Technical term for coloring. In "tipped" cats only the tips

of the hairs are darker than the rest of the fur.

Tomcats' singing
This is wrongly called a love song, but it is really the threatening song of two opponents who are eye to eye with each other. The rising and falling wailing is interspersed with deep rumbling snarls.

Tortoiseshell cats
Name for tricolored cats in black, red, cream, or white. They are considered to be LUCKY CATS. The tricoloration is coupled with the female gene. Tortoiseshell tomcats are extraordinarily rare and then usually are sterile.

Train travel
Cats may travel on a railroad if they are in a closed basket or travel carrier. It goes without saying that the cat travels along with you in the compartment and not in the baggage car, where it literally would be frightened to death.

Treading
See KNEADING.

Trust
Trust of humans is taught the kitten by its mother. We then have the obligation to confirm this trust with love, stroking, and play. Punishment, injustice, confusion, and noise, on the other hand, will severely damage it if not destroy it entirely forever.

U

Undercoat
The term for the thick, soft woolly fur under the cover hairs that also occurs in different thicknesses in various breeds. In Chartreuse and Russian Blues the undercoat is as long as the cover coat so that we speak of a double coat (see pages 135 and 128).

V

Valerian
Works on cats the way hash-ish does on people. They usually go into ecstasy when they get it to smell or to taste (see CATNIP).

Variety
Subspecies of a breed, particularly a special color form.

Vitamins
Of vital importance to the body maintenance of the cat (see page 50).

Vomiting
Cats vomit rather often, for instance if they've eaten too fast. Also, they have to vomit the hair they've swallowed with licking, or hair balls will develop in their intestinal tracts (see BEZOARS). Eating grass promotes the vomiting of hair balls. When vomiting is accompanied by diarrhea, listlessness, and fever, or if there is blood in the vomitus, the cat must be taken to the veterinarian at once.

W

Weaning
The switch from mother's milk to solid food is managed by the mother cat alone. But you can help her if after three to four weeks you feed the kittens small quantities of chopped meat, cooked fish without bones, or prepared baby food.

Weighing
Because cats will not stand on a scale by themselves, the problem is solved by standing on the scale oneself while holding the cat and then subtracting one's own weight.

Whiskers
The coarse hairs the cat has on its upper lip, over the eyes, and on its front legs. With the help of these sensory organs, the cat can even find its way in the dark and catch and kill its prey. Besides cats can tell if they can fit through a narrow opening. In anger and excitment, the cat lays its whiskers back.

Wildcat
See EUROPEAN WILDCAT.

Leaping over the brook. No problem for an experienced jumper. Cats overcome the obstacles they encounter outdoors in their own elegant way.

112

Portraits of Favorite Purebred Cats

Cats are wonderful animals, whether it is "only" the ordinary house cat or a purebred cat with a pedigree that includes several champions in the last four generations. Still, for many cat fanciers these purebred specimens are just the most elegant, most unfathomable, most lovable, most enchanting creatures in the world. In addition there are a few mysterious stories entangled with the beginnings of some breeds.

The Origin of the Breeds

The first breeds originated through mutation (spontaneous genetic change that is consistently passed on to offspring), through which the color, coat, and configuration were altered. Such a "whim of nature" is credited with the beginning of the oldest cat breed, the Turkish Angora (see page 122). Because this cat also could reproduce only within its own breed, the characteristic qualities that made it into an Oriental long-haired cat were established. When the first specimens of these cats reached England and France from Turkey in the sixteenth century, they were much admired bcause of their silvery, silky coats. In time, different types developed among the long-haired cats and when people gave first preference to the cat with the more compact body build and the thick, fine fur, the Persian cat breed began.

Cat Breeders' Associations and the Standard

It began as a hobby—and now the breeding of purebred cats has grown into a very serious affair. After cats were shown at an exhibition for the first time in 1871 in England, the cat breeders formed a club and laid down guidelines for judging that constitute the rules for cat breeders' associations even to this day. Briefly, they are concerned with the purity of the breed and its different varieties, their classification, the entries in the studbook, and the recognition of the national clubs as the highest authority in all questions about the breed.

The international commission of judges of the cat breed associations also established the Standard for all cat breeds. This is the description of the "ideal" animal of a breed.

The United States has eight governing bodies, of which the Cat Fanciers' Association, Inc. (CFA) is by far the largest, with many affiliated cat clubs. Besides establishing the different cat standards, the CFA trains and appoints judges, authorizes shows across the country, controls a nationwide scoring system in its affiliated clubs' shows, and publishes the excellent *CFA Yearbook*.

Other important governing bodies are the American Cat Association (the oldest one in the United States), the American Cat Fanciers' Association, Inc., The Cat Fanciers' Federation, Inc., the Crown Cat Fanciers' Federation, and the United Cat Federation, Inc.

These groups cooperate with each other and with the Canadian Cat Association, so it is now possible for Canadian cats to enter shows in the United States and vice versa. The CFA also cooperates with the FIFE (Fédération Internationale Féline d'Europe), and the two organizations use each other's judges.

Cat Beauties Introduced

In spite of their lofty origins, the purebred cats introduced in the following section are regular cats. Extreme expressions of breed characteristics that some breeders have developed—streamlined Siamese, Persians without noses, naked or tailless cats—falsify the picture of the cat as drawn in this book.

Predator cat. Since the wild fallow cat attached itself to human beings 3500 years ago, it has changed little and retained much of its wild heritage.

Persian

Above: Persian, golden shaded, male one and one-half years.
Below: Color point, blue point, female, two years*
Opposite page:
Above left: Persian, red, male, ten months.
Above right: Chinchilla, female, four years.
Below: Blue smoke, nine weeks.

The mixture of baby face with large, shining saucer eyes, and the uniquely beautiful coat and sweet nature have made this into one of the most popular purebred cats. It is thought that the Persian developed from the long-haired cat from Angora (Ankara). The English began to systematically develop the more compact type with a broader head, short ears, and flatter face.

Body Build: Large to medium large. Compact and muscular, powerful bone structure. Legs short, sturdy.
Coat: Long and thick, fine texture (not woolly). Because of the well-developed undercoat, it is full and fluffy. A projecting "lion's mane" envelops the chest and neck.
Colors: Almost no other breed is bred in such a variety of colors as the Persian.
Single color: Same color evenly all over without any light shading.
Black: Deep raven black to the roots of the hair. *Chocolate:* All shades of brown. *Lilac:* Color hard to describe, something like milk with a shot of coffee in it and has a rosy shimmer. *White:* Absolutely pure white. *Blue:* Is in reality a gray with a bluish shimmer. *Red:* Deep, dark, warm red. Very difficult to breed. *Cream:* Pastel-colored. *Black, Smoke, Cameo, Shell, Shaded:* Silver-white undercoat, the tips of the hairs in the particular color, just as with all the tortoiseshell variations. For instance in black smoke, the hair tips are black

and so distributed that the fur appears "smoked" or sooty.

Silver Striped or Silver Tabby: Basic color: pure, tipped silver with contrasting marking in the color.

Striped (Tabby): Basic color somewhat lighter, shot through with distinct, contrasting darker stripes of the same color. A distinct "M" should be visible on the forehead.

Tortoiseshell, Tortoiseshell and White: The colors red and black or blue and cream and so forth must be well distinguished from one another in spots and be separated. In combination with white at least one half must be colored.

Bicolor: The colored areas should be clearly delineated from the white and be evenly distributed on both sides of the body. In the *Harlequin,* the colored areas are found only on the face and on the tail.

Colorpoint: Masking like the Siamese cat.

Chinchilla: Undercoat pure white.

Back, flanks, head, ears, and tail are lightly tipped in the designated color. Eyes rimmed with the tipping color.

Golden: Undercoat a warm cream. Fur on back, flanks, head, and tail so strongly tipped with dark brown that cat appears golden. Colors are distinguished as golden shell and golden shaded.

Head: Large, broad, and round; full cheeks. Ears small, rounded, widely separated from each other and furnished with attractive tufts of hair. The small, short, broad nose has a distinct

"stop," that is, a deep indentation at the base of the nose.

Eyes: Large, round, and open— "saucer eyes." In most of the colors: copper or dark orange. In white: blue or one blue and one orange (odd-eyed). In silver striped, golden, and chinchilla: green; in colorpoint: blue.

Tail: Short and bushy, slightly rounded at the tip, with a fringe on the underside.

Disposition: The Persian's imperturbability is legendary. But with some color varieties you do find some quite lively cats. Among these are chinchillas, colorpoint, silver, golden, red, tortoiseshell, and black.

Affectionate, sociable, and tolerant by nature, Persians are ideal family and house cats. But they love to go outside if they are given the opportunity.

Suitable for: People who are looking for a majestic, imposing, quiet breed for the house.

Of special note: Require a great deal of grooming.

Persian Color Varieties

Tortoiseshell on white, female, eighteen months.

Cream, female, two years.

Black-and-white, female, four months.

Chocolate ticked, female with six-week-old kitten.

Chocolate tortoiseshell, female, one year.

Black, female, one year.

Bicolor, male, eighteen months.

Harlequin, male three years.

Silver striped, male, six months.

Daily combing and brushing is necessary for Persian cats because otherwise the fur becomes so tangled and matted that the cat finally must be shorn by the veterinarian. Regular powdering and bathing adds to the grooming. Anyone who has a Persian with the very typical shallow, compressed face eventually must reckon with health problems: tearing eyes, breathing problems, birth difficulties from the extremely broad head and in biting off the umbilical cord, sometimes even problems with eating.

Maine Coon

Above: Maine Coon, black tabby with agouti, male, three years, Below: Blue silver tabby, five weeks.*

The Maine Coon is an original breed that has developed independently chiefly in the State of Maine. Probably it came from the semi-longhairs (either Norwegian Forest Cats or Turkish Angoras) that were brought to America by sailors and that mated with the native cats. The name coon reflects the resemblance of its coat to the raccoon's.

Body Build: Medium-sized to very large. Tomcat can weigh up to 22 pounds (10 kg). Powerful with broad chest. Body shape elongated and rectangular.
Coat: Thick, falling loosely. Soft, fine undercoat with coarse, smooth cover hairs. Short on the shoulders, longer on the belly and back legs. Lush neck ruff desirable; tufts of fur between paws. Length and thickness of coat varies with the time of year and the climate.
Colors: All colors and markings except for Siamese points, chocolate, and lilac. "Classic" Maine coon color is tabby, popular with white bib and white paws.
Head: Wedge-shaped, broad, with slanting contour of the muzzle. Strong chin, medium-long nose, and large ears with thick tufts of hair.
Eyes: Large, round, slightly slanting and widely spaced. Colors: Green, golden-orange; in white: blue or odd-eyed.
Tail: As long as the body. Broad at the base, tapering to a point. Long, wavy fur; bushy when the tail is raised.
Disposition: Even, sociable, and peaceable. Can be really affectionate and playful but retains its independence.
Suitable for: People who are looking for a robust, easy-to-care-for semi-long-haired cat that also gets along well with children. Maine coons can be kept in the house but they love a terrace or exercise in the yard.
Of special note: All colors of its heavy shaggy coat are possible, and the eyes are supposed to match the color of the cat.

Norwegian Forest Cat

Body Build: Medium-sized, powerful, long, and supple. The rear legs are longer than the front legs.

Coat: Long and thick. The undercoat is overlaid with glossy, water-repellent hairs. Long neck ruff, beard, "knickerbockers" on the back legs and tufts on the ears. The summer coat is usually shorter.

Colors: All colors permitted.

Head: The long nose without a stop should form a triangle with the widely set ears (in contrast to the Maine coon with its broad, slanting head and not very long nose).

Eyes: Large and open. The color matching the fur.

Tail: Long and very bushy.

Disposition: Friendly and uncomplicated and thus lively and playful. It is a dexterous climber and it invites its owner's affection in a soft voice. Norwegians love children, are very sociable and peaceable, and therefore can be integrated well into a preexisting group of cats. Because of its social nature the Norwegian is seldom really happy when kept as a single cat.

Suitable for: People who are looking for an unspoiled breed of long-haired purebred cat that, like the Maine coon, can get by with a thorough brushing once a week. During the shedding season, however, they can lose a tremendous amount of hair.

Of special note: Norwegians love to be outside in any weather. Their water-repellent coat protects them from damp and cold. The very house tiger itself, happy and always on the terrace, even if the sun isn't shining at all.

Left: Norwegian Forest Cat, black-and-white, female, four and one-half years,
Right: Black tortie tabby with white, female, four and one-half years*.

The Norwegian forest cat, "Norsk Skaukatt," is a true child of nature from the far North. A long-haired farm cat that has been at home in the fjords and dark forests of its homeland for centuries. Its water-repellent coat with its warm undercoat protects it from rain and snow. Recently the friendly, uncomplicated Norwegian also has taken possession of our households and is finding more and more enthusiastic admirers.

Turkish Angora or Ankara Cat

Above: Turkish Angora, white, female, one and one-half years*, Below: White and cream white, four and one-half weeks.

A very old breed of semi-long-haired beauties that originated naturally in Turkey. Named for the city of Angora (now Ankara), the white angora exclusively is considered the only genuine one by many cat fanciers, even today, although in Turkey this cat is found in many colors. The first Angoras arrived in England and France in the sixteenth century; in America, not until the late 1960s.

Body Build: Medium-sized, long, and delicate-limbed. Rear legs somewhat longer than the front legs. Chest slightly protruding. The movements graceful and very lithe.

Coat: Very fine and silkily glossy—no undercoat. Medium long on the body, neck ruff desirable, softly wavy on the belly.

Colors: White is still always the most preferred color, but all the other colors of long-haired cats exist.

Head: Wedge-shaped, broad at the top, tapering to a point at the chin. Medium-long nose without a stop. Large, pointed ears with tufts.

Eyes: Large, almond-shaped, slightly upward-slanting.
White cats: Blue, golden, or odd-eyed.
Other coat colors: Amber-yellow to yellow-green.

Tail: Long and full, tapering to a point.

Disposition: Friendly, lively, and playful. Not so "talkative" as other Orientals.

Suitable for: People who want a very elegant, Oriental-looking cat with graceful movements. Nevertheless this cat is no creation for the luxury market but a breed that has remained natural.

Of special note: Coat care is less demanding than for the Persian because without an undercoat, the fur is less inclined to mat. But the loss of hair is more pronounced during shedding. White cats with blue eyes can be born deaf.

Turkish Van

As with the Turkish Angora, the Van is a breed that originated naturally. It first reached England from the mountains around Lake Van, in Turkey, in the 1960s. Unusual about the breed are the rare chestnut-red markings and the fact that, in its habitat, this cat likes to swim in shallow water.

Body Build: Medium-heavy, muscular type, long but rather compact.

Coat: Chalk-white, without a trace of yellow. On the face, chestnut-red spots in the ear area. The ears themselves must be pure white. The tail is likewise chestnut red, with somewhat darker rings of the same color.

Head: Short triangle, blunted at the bottom. Medium-length straight nose, strong chin, powerful neck. Broad at the base, ears slightly round at the top, heavily furred.

Eyes: Large, round to slightly oval. Bright amber. The lids should be rimmed with pink.

Tail: Furry without undercoat. Medium-long.

Disposition: A quite spirited cat that loves to tear through the house with other companions. Likes to be the first fiddle in a group. Loves exercise in the yard but also can be kept in the house.

Suitable for: People who like a natural cat that occasionally can be quite headstrong. Nevertheless the Van is very devoted to its owner, likes attention without any pressure.

Of special note: This breed likes water and loves to swim.

It does not follow, however, that all the Van cats bred in Europe share this passion. Leave it to your cat to decide whether or not it wants to go into the water. Van cats are still quite rare in this country.

Javanese and Balinese

Left: Javanese, Havana (smoke), female, two years, Right: Balinese, Seal point, male, one and one-half years*, Below: Balinese, Blue point, twelve weeks.

The Javanese arose from the semi-long-haired descendants of a breed that is really a shorthair, the Siamese line. On the other hand, the Javanese comes from crossing the Balinese and the Oriental Shorthair. These breeds, still very new and rare, have nothing to do with the islands of the same names. Probably they reminded the American breeder of the gracefulness of temple dancers. The Standard for the Balinese resembles that of the Siamese, for the Javanese that of the Oriental Shorthair. The single difference is the longer coat.

Body Build: Long and graceful with firm musculature. The slender legs are longer in the back than in the front. The hips are never broader than the shoulders.

Coat: Medium-long, fine, and very silky without undercoat.

Colors: *Balinese:* All Siamese colors (see page 131). *Javanese:* All colors of the Oriental Shorthair (see page 132).

Head: Long, wedge shape of medium size. The long, straight nose should be extended without a stop, the forehead flat. The neck is slender and long, the ears strikingly large, pointed, and broad at the base.

Eyes: Almond-shaped, must not squint. *Balinese:* Shining, deep blue. *Javanese:* Green, but with a white coat deep-blue.

Tail: Long, tapering to a fine point, with outspread hairs.

Disposition: Somewhat more temperate in disposition than the Siamese but with a powerful drive to be active. Devoted and affectionate, they respond very sensitively and are extraordinarily intelligent.

Suitable for: People who enjoy a gracefully elegant, very lively, and also demanding cat.

Of special note: Becomes sexually mature early, raises its young devotedly. Easy to care for.

Somali

Above: Somali, wild color, female, ten months,
Below left: Blue silver, three months,
Below right: Blue, five months.

Somalis don't come from the African country of the same name at all. Rather, they are a created breed that was developed from the Abyssinians. The Americans and the Australians bred them to produce this very beautiful new breed, which was officially recognized in Europe in 1981.

Body Build: Medium-sized, the male clearly larger and sturdier. Lithe, graceful, but with well-developed musculature. The back is slightly arched and gives the impression that the animal is read to spring.

Coat: Medium-length, shorter at the shoulders. Cats with long "trouserlets" and well-developed neck ruffs are preferred.

Colors: Ruddy (orange-brown tipped with black) and red (red tipped with brown). Born dark, Somalis need about two years for the coat to be completed.

Head: Slightly rounded wedge shape, large broad ears.

Eyes: Large, slightly almond-shaped and expressive. Clear, intense amber yellow or green. Dark lids with somewhat darker edges.

Tail: Long and bushy.

Disposition: Very playful and lively, affectionate, and extremely peaceable. Can be kept easily with other cats. Climbs and springs enthusiastically.

Suitable for: Owners who would like to have a lively yet even-tempered cat.

Of special note: Because of the ticked fur, this cat has an air of wildness; the sorrel Somalis with their bushy tails resemble little foxes. These semi-long-haired cats scarcely shed at all.

Birman, Sacred Cat of Burma

Above: Birma, Seal point, male, one year,*
Below left: Blue point, female, five and one-half months,
Below right: Seal point, seven weeks.

The Birman owes its epithet "sacred" to a legend that supposedly the soul of a murdered priest in one of the temples of Birma (formerly Burma) entered into the animal. However, it is improbable that the Birman is native to Southeast Asia. France is today thought to be the country where it was bred, probably a cross of Siamese, European Shorthair, and Persian.

Body Build: Medium-heavy and slightly elongated, legs short and sturdy.

Coat: Semi-long to long, even short on some parts of the body, the face for example, full neck ruff. Altogether the coat is not as long as the Persian's.

Colors: The same characteristic markings (points) on face, ears, feet, and tail as with the Siamese. Most commonly occurring: Seal point (dark brown) or blue point (blue-gray). The rest of the coat: Light eggshell color, the back golden-beige, the belly completely white. Breed characteristics: four white "gauntlets" on the feet (see Of special note).

Head: Sturdy skull, nose without stop, well-proportioned without "Persian" or "Siamese" effect.

Eyes: Blue.

Tail: Thickly feathered, bushy at the end.

Disposition: In temperament, a mixture of quiet Persian and lively Siamese. A lovable, friendly cat that needs close human contact. Sociable as it is, the Birman enjoys living with other cats and pets. Melodious voice.

Suitable for: Families with children, a single person who is at home a great deal. Ideal apartment cat, because it isn't driven to be out of doors.

Of special note: When happy it carries its tail curled over its back like a squirrel. Unique: All four paws have white "gauntlets," which end at the base of the toes or at the ankle. In the back feet the white should go to a point. Birmans only need be brushed now and then because their fur isn't inclined to become matted.

Ragdoll

Body Build: Medium large to large, sturdy and muscular. Only fully grown at four years. Tomcat weighs up to 22 pounds (10 kg).
Coat: Medium long to long, full neck ruff with upstanding "bib," texture plushy and silky.
Colors: *Colorpoint:* Points (markings) on ears, face, legs, and tail. Frost point, blue point, chocolate point, and seal point (see Siamese, page 131).
Bicolor: Mask with upside-down white V, belly, legs, paws, and neck ruff white. Points as above.
Mitted: Points with white blotches, white "mittens" in front and long, white "boots" in the back.
Head: Broad, wedge-shaped, nose with moderate stop. Neck short and sturdy.
Eyes: Large, slightly oval. Blue, the more luminous the better.
Tail: Long, sturdy, and bushy.
Disposition: Extraordinarily gentle and patient, but not at all phlegmatic, although because of their size and weight are not such good hunters, as, say, the graceful Oriental breeds. They take in the goings on around them with interest but with composure. Ragdolls are the ideal apartment cats, because they feel best within their own four walls and only rarely want to go outside.
Suitable for: Families with children, other cats, and pets, because the Ragdoll is sociable and very peaceable.
Of special note: When picked up, the ideal Ragdoll should let head and feet hang down loosely like a ragdoll. But this animal is no ragdoll or plush toy.

Left to right: Ragdoll: Seal Color point, female, three years; Seal bicolor, female, four years; Blue mitted, male, four years.

Again and again you hear the silly story about the origin of the Ragdoll, which has only wronged this gentle-natured, beautiful cat. Because the ancestress, a white Persian cat, was in an automobile accident while pregnant, all her descendants were supposed to be unable to stand pain and be incapable of fighting. Of course this is utter nonsense! On the contrary, all genetically pure Ragdolls go back to a white long-haired cat named Josefine and the tomcat Raggedy. Bred in the United States since about 1960, this breed is still very rare in Europe.

Russian Blue

Russian Blue, female, two years*.

Perhaps the Czar did have the slender blue Russian with the green eyes at his court. It is established that this cat did cross the seas to England from Archangelsk (Russia) in the middle of the last century. People also call these cats Maltese or Spanish Blue, which implies a broader distribution. Unfortunately this very beautiful breed has become quite rare and through many crossings, sometimes with the slender Siamese, sometimes with the sturdy British Blue, so ununiform in appearance that visitors to cat shows today frequently confuse it with the blue Oriental or blue Burmese.

Body Build: Elongated and long-legged with moderately sturdy bone structure. Overall impression is one of grace.

Coat: Short, thick, very fine and soft, plushily fluffy like seal or beaver fur. Texture and appearance of coat are real identifying characteristics of this breed.

Colors: Pure, even blue-gray with silver-tipped lead hairs, which lend the coat the silvery shimmer typical for this breed. Medium blue-gray is preferred. The Russian Blue owes its name to this color.

Head: Short and wedge-shaped. Medium-length nose, sturdy chin, and strongly accentuated whisker cushion. Ears large and pointed; insides slightly hairy. The long, graceful neck accentuates the elegance of this cat.

Eyes: Large and almond-shaped, set far apart. From emerald-green to bottle-green.

Tail: As long as possible, straight and smooth. Tapering to a point at the end, in contrast to the British and European Shorthairs whose tails are rounded at the end.

Disposition: Varies greatly according to which bloodline is dominant. Sometimes rather lively and demonstratively affectionate if there is still much Siamese blood present, otherwise rather moderate in temperament.

Suitable for: Cat lovers who want a blue cat that likes to cuddle, "speaks" with a person, and can be kept well indoors. In general this cat is not so happy in a very turbulent household.

Of special note: The coat is unique to this breed. It is double—that is, the usually shorter undercoat is exactly as long as the cover hairs. To keep the plushy quality, the fur should not be smoothed with brush and comb and laid flat. Use a coarse-grained powder for grooming, brushing the fur against the grain and then rubbing the cat down gently afterwards with a chamois or a silk cloth.

Abyssinian

Body build: Medium-sized, long and slender, overall effect athletic.
Colors: *Ticking:* Two or three bands of color on each hair. This produces a wild coloration, also called agouti. *Wild colors:* Warm brown/orange, ticking black. *Sorrel:* Shining copper-red, ticking red-brown. *Blue:* Warm blue-gray, ticking steel-blue. *Beige-fawn:* Dull beige, ticking dark cream. *Silver:* Undercoat shining silver white, ticking in the particular color.
Head: Moderately wedge-shaped, strong chin, nose medium-length. Ears quite large and far apart; ear tufts desirable. The neck is delicate.
Eyes: Almond-shaped, large and expressive. Amber to green. Dark eye-rims.
Tail: Sturdy at the base, long and tapering to a point.
Disposition: Friendly and receptive to people, very intelligent and teachable. Many abbies retrieve and can learn all sorts of

tricks. These spirited cats that delight in movement certainly can be kept in an apartment but they absolutely do need something for climbing and leaping. They love balconies and exercise in a yard with trees.
Suitable for: A person who is ready to get involved with this cat. Abyssinians need to be spoken to a great deal or they withdraw and pine away.
Of special note: No other breed so resembles the African fallow cat as does the wild-colored Abyssinian.

Above left: Abyssinian, wild color, female, six months, Above right: Red, male, six months, Below: Wild color, eleven weeks.

The Abyssinian is regarded as the descendant of the cats of the pharaohs. The original breed was probably the African fallow cat, which not only was at home in the Nile valley but also in Abyssinia (modern Ethiopia) among other places. The first cat of this kind reached England in 1860. Thus began the triumphal march of the enigmatic sphinx in puma's clothing, whose admirers even today say of it: "It's not simply a matter of a cat, but of Her Majesty the Cat."

Burmese

Above left: Burma, brown, female, three and one-quarter years,
Above right: Lilac, male, one and one-half years,*
Below: Lilac and chocolate, twelve weeks.

According to legend, these cats stem from a monastery in Burma, where they were kept and honored. In 1930 an American brought the first brown Burmese, named Wong Mau, from Rangoon to the United States. Here she was mated with a Siamese and today is considered the mother of the breed. In the United States, the Burmese is the most popular short-haired breed after the Siamese.

Body build: Of medium size and length. Graceful but muscular and compact. Legs relatively slender.
Coat: Very short and fine, scarcely any undercoat. It lies close and shining.
Colors: With all Burmese the underside of the body must be somewhat lighter than the back and legs. Except on young animals, stripes are not permitted. The classic Burmese color is brown. But they also occur in: blue, chocolate, lilac, red, cream,

chocolate-, seal-, blue-, and lilac-tortie (color description, see Oriental Shorthair, page 132).
Head: A short, stubby wedge-shape, accentuated chin, powerful jaw. Ears widely set, broad at base, tips rounded.
Eyes: Large, very expressive, widely spaced. Almond-shaped, lower eye line rounded, in contrast to the Siamese. Bright yellow to amber.
Tail: Medium long, not thick at base; tapering to a rounded point.
Disposition: Like the Siamese very possessive of its human. A self-assured cat personality that very seldom will submit and mostly has to be leader in a group of cats.
Suitable for: People who want an intelligent, self-confident cat. Loves to ride in cars.
Of special note: Burmese achieve sexual maturity early and have a strong drive. A female in heat develops such a powerful voice that rest and sleep become impossible.

Siamese

Body build: Medium-sized, elongated. A very slender cat with lithe movements.
Coat: Very short, fine, and smooth-lying. With a silky shine.
Colors: Light on the body (white, ivory to beige). Light shading on the flanks permitted. The typical Siamese markings (points) are found on the face, the ears, feet, legs, and tail. *Marking colors, point in:* Seal (dark brown), blue (blue-gray), chocolate (milk-chocolate color), lilac (magnolia color), red (red-gold), cream (cream). In addition this whole palette can exist in tortie point and tabby point. Tortie (mottled), tabby (striped).
Head: Wedge-shaped with long, straight nose. Ears large and pointed.
Eyes: Almond-shaped, slightly slanting. Deep, shining blue. A slight squint appears.
Tail: Long, thin at the base, pointed. Kinks are no longer permitted.
Disposition: Very lively, active,

intelligent, and witty. No chest of drawers or tree is too high, no door with "nibbles" behind it that cannot be opened. Usually this cat has the whole household firmly in hand and obviously any other cats as well. It is extraordinarily communicative, and there are some Siamese owners who "converse" with their cats. Whenever the Siamese is hungry, angry, anxious, or in heat, it develops the vocal power of an operatic diva.
Suitable for: People with much cat sense and experience. Not a beginner's cat. The Siamese is very attached to people and sensitive. If it is badly treated or even given away, the Siamese suffers more psychic damage than other cats.
Of special note: Extreme courses of breeding have so much altered these cats' appearance and disposition that the once very popular Siamese of cat lovers is no longer so prized.

Left: Siamese, Chocolate point, male, one year,
Right: Red point, female, three and one-half years*.

In the Thai National Library in Bangkok there is probably the oldest cat book in the world, which originated in Siam's ancient capital city of Ayudha (1350–1767). Even at that time it described a light cat with dark tail, feet, and ears. Siamese cats from Bangkok were exhibited in London for the first time in 1871 and received the name Royal Siam Cat.

Oriental Shorthair

Above left: Oriental Shorthair, Havana, male, one and one-half years,*
Above right: Lavender self, female, two years,
Below: Chocolate point and chocolate smoke, ten weeks.
Opposite page:
Above left: Chocolate golden spotted, female, three years,*
Above right: Ebony, female, seven months,
Below: Chocolate golden spotted, seven weeks.

Strictly speaking, these cats are single-colored and patterned Siamese without the typical Siamese points. The breed has been in existence for centuries. Old Thai texts describe not only the typical Siamese but also single-colored and bicolored slender Oriental cats. In 1962 systematic breeding was begun in England. In the United States, the Oriental Shorthair wasn't recognized until the mid-seventies.

Body build: Medium-sized and elongated. Like the Siamese a very slender cat with fluid movements and exuding elegance.
Coat: Very short, fine, and smooth-lying. Silkily glossy.
Colors: *Single-colored:* Havana (warm, uniform chestnut-brown), blue (pure light to medium blue-gray), lavender (pale lavender-blue with a distinct pink shimmer), ebony (gleaming deep black to the roots of the hairs), red (warm red, tabby-pattern as faint as possible), cream (warm, light apricot), foreign white (pure

white, without any shading).
Tortoiseshell: Black tortie, blue tortie, chocolate tortie, lilac tortie. In all of these, the particular background color is as clear and bright as possible, red and/or cream so distributed over the body that it gives a shaded effect. A red or cream-colored flame on the ridge of the nose is desirable.
Tabby: Can be mackerel, striped, blotched, or spotted. Ticked (agouti, with and without silver in all colors). Contrasting markings; on a lighter background. In the ticked-tabby the rump is completely free of markings, only its extremities show a strong striped pattern. In all tabbies a prominent "M" on the forehead is desirable.
Smoke: Light platinum-colored undercoat, the tips of the hairs and the short-haired body parts (face, ears, legs) appear faintly or strongly pigmented, depending on the genes for color, in the entire range of colors discussed above.

Head: Medium-sized, well proportioned in relation to body. Wedge-shaped; the ears are large, pointed, broad at the base and extend the sides of the wedge. The nose is thin. The neck is long and slender.

Eyes: Almond-shaped, slightly slanting. Green in all Oriental Short-hairs. Only blue in foreign white.

Tail: Very long, thin at the base, ends in a point.

Disposition: Very similar to the Siamese, especially when it is an "extreme type." Otherwise, in everything else, even the voice, somewhat more subdued—particularly for the Havanas, the lavender, and the ebony, which are also pictured here. All Orientals are full of spirit and in an apartment absolutely need sufficient room for activity, otherwise furniture, curtains, and carpets will suffer all too much: scratching posts, a secure terrace with places to climb, and also exercise in the yard when the sun is shining. Like the

Siamese, the Orientals are superb mousers. Unfortunately birds also are not safe from them. They love warmth and, more than other cats, like to lie in the sun or sleep directly over the radiator. That they are devotedly attached, full of chatter, and very human-oriented betrays their close relationship to the Siamese. The Oriental Shorthairs often can be walked on a leash and love being around where something is going on. Because they are very curious, being penned in is a torture for them.

Suitable for: Experienced cat keepers and sensitive people who are ready to give this cat much attention, time, and love. Families with small children should get a more patient cat instead—which does not mean that the Oriental Shorthair and the Siamese don't like children. Quite the contrary, but they don't tolerate rough handling and can be really resentful. As very social cats, they live well in a group, best with breeds that are not as dominating as they are. Such a mixture of breeds also brings somewhat more peace into the cats' lives, which is a very noticeable advantage.

Of special note: Siamese and Orientals can mate with each other and often do. Thus the kittens of a litter may be either only Siamese or only Orientals or a mixture of the two breeds. If an Oriental Shorthair has yellow-green eyes, it can be crossed with a blue-eyed Siamese to get the unique "witch's eyes."

133

Scottish Fold

Above: Scottish Fold, blue-white cream, female, three and one-half years,
Below: Blue-white, of a litter with folded-eared and normal-eared kittens, four weeks.

After a folded-eared cat appeared by mutation on a farm in Clackmanshire, Scotland, in 1961, and this cat by the name of Susie also bore lop-eared kittens, the shepherd there began to breed her. But through too much inbreeding and bad crossing, deaf and blind kittens as well as stillbirths occurred. The British cat society therefore outlawed the breed, and later the Americans awakened it to new life. Today, for security, these cats are usually mated with Persians, British, American, or European Shorthairs. All in all, these cats are very robust and healthy.

Body build: Medium-sized and strong, comparable to the British Shorthair.
Coat: Short, thick, soft, and graspable.
Colors: All colors except chocolate, lilac, and Siamese markings.
Head: Beautifully round with prominent chin, jaw, and full cheeks. The small ears folded forward lend the face a rather helpless and babylike look.
Eyes: Large and round. Color depends on coat color.
Tail: Medium-long, thick at the base.

Disposition: Lovable, friendly cats that get along well both with people and other animals. It's a very good, clean apartment cat.
Suitable for: People who are pleased by such an unusual cat.
Of special note: The folded ear, the characteristic feature for this breed, arises from a fold in the outer edge of the ear, which causes the tip of the ear to bend over. With normal care and maintenance these cats are no more susceptible to ear mites and ear infections than those with upstanding ears. The young Scottish Fold kittens appear completely "normal" at birth. It only shows about the third week of life who in the litter, which is always a mixture, is going to be a cat with folded ears or upstanding ones. Other cats always have misunderstandings at first because of this particular ear placement. In cat language, flattened ears mean anger and displeasure. It takes a while for them to realize that their companion always looks this way.

British Shorthair, Chartreuse

Above: Chartreuse, British Shorthair blue, male, two years*, Below: Black-and-silver striped, male, two years*.

English house cats, paired with Persians, were the parent animals of the modern British Shorthair breed. The so-called Chartreuse cats have been included in the family as British Blue since the changed Standard of 1980. The original French Chartreuse are scarcely seen in the large shows in our day. In this way they share the fate of the Russian Blue. Still, this confusion doesn't harm the popularity of the British Shorthair by any means; the blue-gray teddy bear, especially, takes people's hearts by storm.

Body build: Medium-sized to large, compact body, massive, sturdy, with broad chest and not very long legs (the "blue," especially, can weigh up to 20 pounds [9 kg]).

Coat: "Double," with heavy undercoat. Very thick and plushy. Slightly upstanding and not close-lying like the other short-haired breeds.

Colors: All hairs must be thoroughly colored to the roots, except for silver and tabby varieties (color description, see Persian, pages 116 and 117).

Head: Broad at the chin with full cheeks. Short, broad nose with slight stop at the base of the nose. Ears medium-sized, on the small side, widely set and placed high. They round off the head at the top.

Eyes: Large and round, "saucer-eyes." Copper or dark orange. In golden or silver varieties: Green eyes.

Tail: Not too long, sturdy. End slightly rounded.

Disposition: "Very British." Provided with a stable nervous system, moves with friendly openness but is very self-assured in its own territory. These cats are not sensitives who "snuggle up" to their people and woo loudly for some tenderness.

They prize well-measured attention and care.

Suitable for: People who want a nice cat but respect that it does not want constant stroking and carrying around. Because of its even temperament you easily can keep this breed with other cats and house pets. Besides they get along well with children, and because they keep their urge to freedom in bounds, they are the ideal apartment cats.

Of special note: Cats that are bred for extreme massiveness and weight can lose their vitality as a result. It's easy to fall in love with cuddly teddy bears the size of dachshunds, nevertheless, as a cat fancier you should give preference to the more moderate type.

Exotic Shorthair

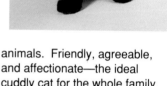

Left: Exotic Shorthair, golden shell, female, two and one-half years*,
Right: Black, male, three and one-half years*.

This plush cat with a babyface comes from crossing a Persian with an American Shorthair, or in England with the British Shorthair. First presented at shows in the United States in the class of nonrecognized cat breeds, it soon was recognized and in the eighties began its conquering march to Europe. It is prized as a breed that has the quiet disposition, the sturdy body build, the dollface and the fluffy coat of the Persian and yet is easy to groom—for many cat fanciers the perfect combination.

Body build: Large to medium-sized, compact and sturdy on short, powerful legs (Persian type).
Coat: Longer than that of the other short-haired breeds. Stands away from the body, very soft, thick, and plushy.
Colors: All the colors permitted in the Persian (see pages 116 and 117).
Head: Round and massive with broad crown. Full cheekbones, very strong jaw and chin. *Nose:* short, blunt, and wide, with a more marked stop than other short-haired breeds.
Eyes: Large, round, shining saucer-eyes; wide open and spaced far apart. As with the Persian, according to coat copper, dark-orange, green, or blue.
Tail: Short and sturdy. Set low without arching.
Disposition: An ideal apartment cat that is attached to its home. Its temperament is rather quiet, moderate. Among golden and silver Exotics you find livelier

animals. Friendly, agreeable, and affectionate—the ideal cuddly cat for the whole family, especially for children.
Suitable for: People who prefer sturdy, compact cats with quiet dispositions, who like the Persian's doll face and the plushy fur for stroking but wish to avoid the daily combing and the tiresome shedding.
Of special note: If the cat has the extremely flat Persian face, it also will have inherited most of the Persian weaknesses: running eyes, difficulty breathing, and so forth. If you give preference, rather, to a less exaggerated type, you later will have correspondingly more pleasure in your short-haired Persian.

Devon, Cornish, German Rex

Body build: *Devon Rex:* Medium-sized, very firm and muscular. Legs long and slender, slightly bowed where joined to the body (O-legs). Broad chest, long, slender neck. *Cornish and German Rex* have the body build of the European Shorthair, but the Cornish is slenderer, like an Oriental.
Coat: Very short, fine, and soft in texture. Wavy or curly like Persian lamb fur. Whiskers and eyebrows curly. The Devon Rex coat has very short, fine, and wavy hairs, which the Cornish and German Rex do not, making their coats soft and velvety to the touch.
Colors: All colors permissible.
Head: *Devon Rex:* Short, wedge-shaped, with prominent cheekbones. Full cheeks. Short muzzle with sturdy chin and "whisker break" (whisker cushion). Broad nose with prominent stop. Low-set, large "bat ears."
Cornish Rex: Moderately Oriental-looking. *German Rex:* Similar to European Shorthair

with rounder, broader head, slight stop and medium-sized ears.
Eyes: *Devon Rex:* Widely spaced, large, almond-shaped. *Cornish Rex:* Oriental almond-eyes. *German Rex:* Corresponding to European Shorthair. Color according to coat color.
Tail: Long, thin, and pointed. Thickly covered with short hair.
Disposition: Ideal, very domestic apartment cat that loves warmth, especially the Devon. Lively in disposition, the Rex has a tendency to clown. The German Rex is not so "Oriental" in temperament but rather more laid back, but just as sweet and affectionate.
Suitable for: All who like a very rare, unusual-looking cat.
Of special note: Immature young animals often have bald places in their fur, especially the Devon. If both parent animals have good coats of fur, this will pass. Rex coats grow slowly and unevenly.

Left: German Rex, tortoiseshell, female, one and one-half years, Right: Devon Rex, smoke, female, seven years.

A unique breed of cats, the Rex has a short, curly coat as a result of a mutation. Probably the first cats of this kind appeared in Germany but were not further regarded. The first cat, Kallibunker, born in Cornwall (England) in 1950, was the ancestor of the modern day Cornish Rex. When a curly-haired kitten appeared again a little later in nearby Devon, the Devon Rex was bred from it, producing what is probably the best known of the three breeds today. The name Rex comes from a rabbit breed of the same name.

Index

Page numbers in **boldface** indicate color photos. **C1** indicates front cover; **C2,** inside front cover; **C3,** inside back cover; and **C4,** back cover.

Addresses and Literature

Cat Clubs

American Cat Association, Inc.
Susie Page
10065 Foothill Boulevard
Lake View Terrace,
California 91342

American Cat Fanciers'
Association, Inc.
Edward Rugenstein
P.O. Box 203
Point Lookout, Missouri
65726

Canadian Cat Association
Donna Aragona
14 Nelson Street W., Suite 5
Brampton, Ontario
Canada L6X 1B7

Cat Fanciers' Association, Inc.
Walter A. Friend, Jr.,
President
1309 Allaire Avenue
Ocean, New Jersey 07712

Cat Fanciers' Federation, Inc.
Barbara Haley
9509 Montgomery Road
Cincinnati, Ohio 45242

Crown Cat Fanciers'
Federation
Martha Underwood
1379 Tyler Park Drive
Louisville, Kentucky 40204

International Cat Association
(ICA)
Bob Mullen
211 East Olive, Suite 201
Burbank, California 91502

United Cat Federation, Inc.
David Young
6621 Thornwood Street
San Diego, California 9211

Books

Behrend, K. *Cats*. Barron's Educational Series, Inc., Hauppauge, New York, 1991.

Frye, Fredric L., DVM. *First Aid for Your Cat*. Barron's Educational Series, Inc., Hauppauge, New York, 1987.

Leyhausen, Paul. *Cat Behavior*. Garland STPM Press, New York, 1979.

Müller, Ulrike. *Longhaired Cats*. Barron's Educational Series, Inc., Hauppauge, New York, 1984.

——. *The New Cat Handbook*. Barron's Educational Series, Inc., Hauppauge, New York, 1984.

——. *Persian Cats*. Barron's Educational Series, Inc., Hauppauge, New York, 1990.

Pond, Grace. *Longhair Cats*. Barron's Educational Series, Inc., Hauppauge, New York, 1984.

Pugnetti, Gino. *Simon & Schuster's Guide to Cats*. Simon & Schuster, New York, 1984.

Viner, Bradley, DVM, *The Cat Care Manual*. Barron's Educational Series, Inc., Hauppauge, New York, 1986.

Magazines

The Cat Fanciers' Almanac
Cat Fanciers' Association
1309 Allaire Avenue
Ocean, New Jersey 07712

Cat Fancy Magazine
P.O. Box 2431
Boulder, Colorado 80321

Cats Magazine
P.O. Box 290037
Port Orange, FL 32129-0037

CFA Yearbook
Cat Fanciers' Association, Inc.
1309 Allaire Avenue
Ocean, New Jersey 07712

The Prize-winning Cats in This Book

Page 116 (below): Persian, "Anjouli," champion;

Page 120 (above): Maine Coon, "Jack vom Schloss Wolperding," international champion;

Page 121 (above right): Norwegian Forest Cat, "Nora Au-Trolls Fjord," international champion;

Page 122 (above): Turkish Angora, "Ziya's Gamza of Turkish Affairs," international champion;

Page 123 (above): Turkish Van, "Hexi von Schneewittchen," international champion;

Page 124 (above right): Balinese, "Zauserich Schao You," champion;

Page 126 (above): Birma, "Cat Bal'oo of Magic Blue," international champion;

Page 128: Russian Blue, "Von Rasputin," European champion;

Page 130 (above right): Burma "Sacharian Boy von München," international champion;

Page 131 (right in photo): Siamese, "Mona vom Schloss Wolperding," international champion (Premior);

Page 132 (above left): Oriental Shorthair, "Amaryll Fair Murphy's Law," champion;

Page 133 (above left): Oriental Shorthair, "Golden Lacrima Schao You," international champion;

Page 135 (above) Chartreuse, British Shorthair, "Ceyetano vom Eagle Rock," international champion;

Page 135 (below): British Shorthair, "Ursus vom Inhauser Moos," international champion;

Page 136 (left): Exotic Shorthair, "Goldkind vom Bayern," champion;

Page 136 (right): Exotic Shorthair, "Exotic Charly," European champion.

The Authors

Katrin Behrend, journalist, editor of books on animals, and author. She has had both house and purebred cats for many years.

Monika Wegler, professional photographer, journalist, and author of books on animals. In recent years her work has concentrated on animal portraits as well as behavior and movement studies of dogs and cats.

Cover photographs:

Front cover: Chartreuse female and kitten.
Back cover: Above left: Maine Coon tomcat.
Above right: White Main Coon female.
Below left: Crouching Abyssinian tomcat.
Below center: Young house cat.
Below right: Persian female.

Acknowledgments

Authors and publisher wish to thank all the cat owners and breeders of the first DEKZV [German Purebred Cat Breed Club], Munich chapter, for their cooperation. Special mention goes to Susanne Böhnisch, Munich, The Neumann Veterinary Practice, Munich, Dr. Wiesner, Munich, and Attorney Reinhard Hahn, Alsbach-Hänlein.

Important Notes

You can receive injury from scratches and bites when handling cats. Get immediate medical attention for such wounds.

Don't overlook having your cat get all the necessary shots and wormings (see pages 60 and 62); otherwise there is a possible danger to the health of both animal and human. Some diseases and parasites can be passed on to humans (see page 63). If your cat exhibits signs of illness (see table, page 70), consult a a veterinarian immediately. If doubtful about yourself, go to your doctor and tell him that you have a cat.

There are people who are allergic to cat hair. If you are unsure, ask your doctor before you get a cat.

There is a chance that the cat can damage other people's property or cause an accident. A covering insurance policy is in your own interest; you should be insured for liability in any case.

All inquiries should be addressed to:
Barron's Educational Series, Inc.
250 Wireless Boulevard
Hauppauge, NY 11788

Library of Congress Catalog Card No. 91-18156

International Standard Book No. 0-8120-4613-7

Library of Congress Cataloging-in-Publication Data

Behrend, Katrin.
   [Katzen. English]
   The complete book of cat care : how to raise a happy and healthy cat / Katrin Behrend and Monika Wegler; translated from the German by Elizabeth D. Crawford.
      p.   cm.
   Translation of: Katzen.
   Includes index.
   ISBN 0-8120-4613-7
   1. Cats. 2. Cats—Behavior.   I. Wegler, Monika.
II. Title.
SF447.B4513 1991
636.8—dc20   91-18156
                                CIP

Printed and Bound in Hong Kong
34   4900   98765

The Kitten Riddle Game:

Page 125

Page 130

Page 135 (above)

Page 118 (middle right)

Page 121

Page 126